VICTORIOUS CHRISTIAN LIVING ESSENTIALS

Needed Tools for End-time Generals

Akinbowale Isaac Adewumi

Scripture quotations are taken from the HOLY BIBLE (KING JAMES VERSION)

Copyright © 2019 Akinbowale Isaac Adewumi

ISBN: 978-1-9994969-2-0

All Rights Reserved.
No part of this publication may be reproduced, distributed, transmitted in any form or by any means, or stored in a data base or retrieval system without the prior written permission of the publisher.

Editing and inner text design layout by Taiwo Adeodu
+2348051106023

DEDICATION

"For whatsoever is born of God overcometh the world: and this is the victory that overcometh the world, even our faith"
(1 John 5:4)

Dedicated to Almighty God and my fellow friends in tribulation.

CONTENTS

Dedication... *iii*

Introduction... *ix*

CHAPTER ONE
X-RAYING THE DEPRAVED HEARTS OF MEN.....13
God Demands Our Hearts................................. 15
Take Away the Stone………………………………..17
Why God Needs Our Hearts?............................. 19.
A Broken and Contrite Heart…………..………….20

CHAPTER TWO
UPON THE MOUNT ZION…………………….. 25
Deliverance on Mount Zion…………………….. 26
Deeds of a Sinner……………………………………28
Deliverance from Sin……………………………. 29
Desire for Salvation……………………………….. 30
Redemptive Power in the Blood of Jesus…………. 32
New Life in Christ………………………………….. 35
Caution Against the Old Lifestyle…………………..40
Clean Hands and a Pure Heart……………………42

CHAPTER THREE
OUR DAILY BREAD……………………………. 47.
The Word 'Bible'…………………………………. 51.

The Symbol of the Bible…….....………………..…....53
CHAPTER FOUR
PERSECUTION AND TEMPTATION……….…... 57
Persecution is Certain……..……………………….... 58
Temptation is Sure………..……………….…………61
CHAPTER FIVE
FRUIT OF THE SPIRIT………………………….….. 65
Love, Joy, Peace, Long-suffering, Gentleness, Goodness, Faith, Meekness, Temperance……..………......…..68
CHAPTER SIX
TRUE DISCIPLESHIP…………………………….…... 73
The Call to Christian Discipleship ……………..…. 75
Definition of Christian Discipleship……………..…...76
The Importance of Christian Discipleship……..…… 76
Prerequisites to Christian Discipleship……….…….. 77
Hindrances to Christian Discipleship……………….78
Rewards of Christian Discipleship……….…….…… 79
CHAPTER SEVEN
THE HOLY SPIRIT POWER……………………..….81
Pre-requisites to the Holy Spirit Baptism…...…..... 82
Purpose of Holy Spirit Baptism………………….…..84.
Promised Power from God…………..……………... 85
CHAPTER EIGHT
DEFINING THE GIFTS OF THE SPIRIT……….….. 87
CHAPTER NINE
DANIEL - AN UNCOMPROMISING BELIEVER….95
Unashamed Boldness……………………….………..97

Uncommon Standard..101
Unparallel Protection..102
Unhindered Persistence.......................................102
Unblemished Faith... 103
Unusual Test.. 104
Immeasurable Blessing...................................... 104
CHAPTER TEN
THE ESSENCE OF PRAYER................................107
Praying Men in the Bible.....................................110
Experiencing and Maintaining a Prayer Life.......... 111
CHAPTER ELEVEN
PRAYER POWER..115
Command to Ask Great Things..........................115
Blessings of Big Prayers......................................117
Importunate Prevailing Prayer...........................118
The Call to Pray by God......................................119.
The Cause for Importunate Prayer....................120
The Cost of Praying Through to Receive Answers...122.
Catalogue of Answered Prayers in the Bible..........123
CHAPTER TWELVE
OUR CALL TO THE GREAT COMMISSION:
LIFESTYLE EVANGELISM.....................................125
Requirements for the Great Commission...............126
Reasons for Obeying the Great Commission..........130
Reward of Obedience to the Great Commission.......131
CHAPTER THIRTEEN
SPIRITUAL GROWTH AND DEVELOPMENT......133

Purpose of Spiritual Growth................................136
Process of Spiritual Growth................................138
Blessings of Spiritual Growth..............................142
CHAPTER FOURTEEN
RIDING ON THE STORMS OF LIFE......................145
Catalogue of Life's Storms..................................148
Conquering Life's Storms...................................160
CHAPTER FIFTEEN
DISCOVERING YOUR PROPHETIC DESTINY........165
Pointers to Prophetic Destiny...........................…..168
Promises Concerning Your Prophetic Destiny……... 171
CHAPTER SIXTEEN
FULFILLING YOUR REDEMPTIVE REVELATIONS..173
Why You Must Fulfil Your Divine Destiny?……….. 174
How Do We Fulfil God's Purpose for Our Lives? … 176.
Destroying the Stronghold of 'NO' in Destiny…..…. 183
Discerning Personal Strongholds……………………. 185
Demolishing Personal Strongholds……………………187
Developing a Destiny-Fulfilling Disposition………..189
Precepts for All...192
Epilogue.. 197
Bibliography.. 199

INTRODUCTION

After conversion, which means deliverance from sin and its consequences, the believer's heart cry should be becoming like Christ. We are expected to mature into His full stature by sustaining consistent victory over sin, satan and the corrupt world system here on earth. In this contraption, the author espoused that the experiences of salvation, sanctification, Holy Ghost baptism power or anointing for exploits in God's Kingdom are the catalysts of the essential principles for a victorious Christian life. This bedrock crystallizes into the Biblical ingredients of awesome possibilities, plausible promises, special giftings, virtuous fruits, spiritual growth and prophetic permutations, which a child of God can tap into and explore to develop their destiny-fulfilling disposition. Hence the essence of this book, 'VICTORIOUS CHRISTIAN LIVING ESSENTIALS.'

There's a race we must run and there's a victory to be won. God's Kingdom is not an all-comers-jamboree; it is a place of eternal righteousness, peace and joy (Romans 14:17). Entry requires fighting and winning wars. God's Kingdom on earth suffers violence and only the ruthlessly violent enters it and stays inside it until the Kingdom of Heaven comes. This is the final consummation of all things when Christ's Kingdom is fully established and all enemies of the Lord are crushed, judged and sentenced. We don't seem to have the choice in this matter. If we fail to march to the war, the enemy will bring the war to us or ambush us. Unless we are ready to fight and really fight hard, our service in the Kingdom will be fruitless and our hope of eternal life will be a joke.

The saints of old were men who prayed and followed the example of Christ in order to fulfil their earthly ministry. They considered it a grievous sin if prayer is neglected. Samuel said, *"… as for me, God forbid that I should sin against the Lord in ceasing to pray for you… "* 1 Samuel 12:23. (Also, read 1 Samuel 2:9, 17; Genesis 32:26; Zechariah 4:6). The greatest means of accessing and appropriating these privileges is prayer.

Furthermore, we also need to develop our faith to make for potency and victory over every life's hurdle and battle, be it temptation, persecution, financial crisis, ill-health or any other common battle that confronts all believers. *"For whatsoever is born of God overcometh the world: and this is the victory that overcometh the world, even our faith."* 1 John 5:4.

The good fight of faith is a fight to protect our existence in the Kingdom, preserve the purity of the Church and promote the work and services we engaged within the household of God. It is a good fight because it's ordered by God, prosecuted with His weapons and fought with His strength to achieve His good purposes, thus making us victorious in our Christian living until we see Jesus face to face.

CHAPTER ONE

X-RAYING THE DEPRAVED HEARTS OF MEN

John 12:40; Daniel 5:20; *"He hath blinded their eyes, and hardened their heart; that they should not see with their eyes, nor understand with their heart, and be converted, and I should heal them... But when his heart was lifted up, and his mind hardened in pride, he was deposed from his kingly throne, and they took his glory from him."*

The depraved heart is a heart that hinders the manifestation of God's glory and power in many lives today. It is a heart that is stony, deceived, proud, hardened, stony and seared in its conscience. Prophet Jeremiah captured it well when he said, *"The heart is deceitful above all things, and desperately wicked: who can know it?"* (Jeremiah 17:9)

Stony Hearts: *"Yea, they made their hearts as an adamant stone, lest they should hear the law, and the words which the LORD of hosts hath sent in his spirit by the former prophets: therefore came a great wrath from the LORD of hosts."* (Zechariah 7:12)

Deceived Hearts: *"He feedeth on ashes: a deceived heart hath turned him aside, that he cannot deliver his soul, nor say, Is there not a lie in my right hand?"* (Isaiah 44:20)

Proud Hearts: *"We have heard the pride of Moab, (he is exceeding proud) his loftiness, and his arrogancy, and his pride, and the haughtiness of his heart… The pride of thine heart hath deceived thee, thou that dwellest in the clefts of the rock, whose habitation is high; that saith in his heart, Who shall bring me down to the ground?"* (Jeremiah 48:29; Obadiah 1:3)

The proud heart is often afraid of change and rarely welcomes development. It makes one to reject anything that is new to his understanding. The arrogant soul claims to know everything already and that is an expression of pride.

Uncircumcised Hearts: *"Ye stiffnecked and uncircumcised in heart and ears, ye do always resist the Holy Ghost: as your*

fathers did, so do ye." (Acts 7:51)
Parents with hardened and uncircumcised hearts miss everlasting life and Heaven and so do their unrepentant children. This is a great warning. I pray whatever our parents had missed, we are not going to miss in Jesus' name.

Blindness of Hearts: *"Having the understanding darkened, being alienated from the life of God through the ignorance that is in them, because of the blindness of their heart"* (Ephesians 4:18). They don't feel guilty at all whatever they do.

Seared Conscience: *"Speaking lies in hypocrisy; having their conscience seared with a hot iron."* (1 Timothy 4:2)

God Demands Our Hearts

"My son, give me thine heart, and let thine eyes observe my ways." (Proverbs 23:26)

The word 'My son' in this scripture doesn't exclude daughters. Males and females are one in Christ Jesus. In Galatians 3:18, it's confirmed that, *"There is neither Jew nor Greek, there is neither bond nor free, there is neither male nor female: for ye are all one in Christ Jesus."* The heart, in Scripture, signifies the seat of the affections, of wisdom and understanding; it is the center of a man's being. The human heart was created to mirror God's own heart and it refers to the soul of a human being that controls the will and emotions. When we were separated from God with hardened hearts, we found it impossible to please Him; hence, we tended towards selfishness, rebellion, sin and so, displeased Him. In Ecclesiastes 7:29, the Bible says, *"Lo, this only have I found, that God hath made man upright; but they have sought out many inventions."*

From the text (Proverbs 23:26), there are three things God revealed:

1. *A deeper relationship with God.* The Lord says, '**My son**' means, God as a Father of all, a Creator, He's addressing men and women everywhere, for in this sense He is the Father of all men. *"For in him we live, and move, and have our being; as certain also of your own poets have said, for we are also his offspring."* (Acts 17:28). But there is a deeper and more intimate sense in which we need to become the children of God." *If ye be willing and obedient, ye shall eat the good of the land."* (Isaiah 1:19)

2. *A request from God.* "**My son, give me**…"The petitioner is God who is asking us to give Him our hearts, which really means our whole life and everything, our whole being. The fact that God seeks us out and then asks for our hearts, or our love, proves His great love for us. "

For God so loved the world, that he gave his only begotten Son, that whosoever believeth in him should not perish, but have everlasting life." (John 3:16)

3. *A requirement from God.* **"Give me your heart."** Before our gifts become acceptable to God, we must have given Him our hearts. Even if we pray and give out our money, God will not accept it us unless we have first given ourselves to Him. *"The sacrifice of the wicked is an abomination to the Lord: but the prayer of the upright is his delight…He that turneth away his ear from hearing the law, even his prayer shall be abomination"* (Proverbs 15:8; 28:9). God owns us and wants our hearts to be the seat of Christ and desires everything in us for His own glory. If we want our prayer answered, we must fulfil His requirements.

Take Away the Stone

"Jesus said, Take ye away the stone …Circumcise yourselves to the LORD, and take away the foreskins of your heart, ye men of Judah and inhabitants of Jerusalem: lest my fury come forth like fire, and burn that none can quench it, because of the evil of your doings." (John 11:39; Jeremiah 4:4)

You ought to take away from your life any transgression, all detestable things, every abomination and whatever corruption because God hates them. This is how miracles happen. There is always preparation to make for you to see the manifestation of the glory of God in your life and ministry which is by taking away the stony heart out of your flesh.

"Then they took away the stone from the place where the dead was laid. And Jesus lifted up his eyes, and said, Father, I thank thee that thou hast heard me." (John 11:41)

You will take away the stone and not allow any part to remain because that is the path to blessings and miracles. God will not do what we ought to do or which we can easily do by ourselves. He does not place adverts for what you or your pocket can do.

There are some things God expects us to do for ourselves, His will must cross our will and prevail over it. For our Lazarus to come alive, we must remove every stone of barrier, unbelief, indifference, ignorance, carnality, disobedience and worldliness. (John 8:24; Acts 16:31; Hebrews 6:12; 2 Peter 3:18; Colossians 3:5-10; Ephesians 6:5; 1 John 2:15-17)

"Then they took away the stone from the place where the dead was laid. And Jesus lifted up his eyes, and said,

Father, I thank thee that thou hast heard me. And I knew that thou hearest me always: but because of the people which stand by I said it, that they may believe that thou hast sent me. And when he thus had spoken, he cried with a loud voice, Lazarus, come forth. And he that was dead came forth, bound hand and foot with graveclothes: and his face was bound about with a napkin. Jesus saith unto them, Loose him, and let him go." (John 11:41-44)

When the Author of Life utters His Word of Life into our lives, the power of death is broken and the quickening power of resurrection takes over to the glory of God.

Why God Needs Our Hearts?

"Sow to yourselves in righteousness, reap in mercy; break up your fallow ground: for it is time to seek the Lord, till he come and rain righteousness upon you... Teach me thy way, O Lord; I will walk in thy truth: unite my heart to fear thy name." (Hosea 10:12; Psalm 86:11)

God wants our hearts in order to transform it (Jeremiah 4:4; Ezekiel 36:25). When a person is genuinely converted through faith in Jesus, a new life begins with God's love manifesting in his heart and extending towards his neighbour. A *transformed heart will* ultimately be resulted in a *transformed life.* And he can easily love his neighbour like himself. (Mark 12:31)

God wants our heart in order to purge and purify it

(Ezekiel 36:26). This involves purging yourself from the affairs of this life - 2 Timothy 2:14; from unbelief - 2 Timothy 2:13; from denying Christ - 2 Timothy 2:12; from fake doctrines that destroy faith - 2 Timothy 2:14, 18; from profane and vain babblings that lead to ungodliness - 2 Timothy 2:16-17; from iniquity and dishonour - 2 Timothy 2:19-20.

God wants our heart fixed on Him in order to empower us (Ezekiel 36:27). The heart is the "inner man." When we are born again, God performs a heart transplant, as it were. He gives us a new heart of flesh. The power of the Holy Spirit changes our hearts from being sin-focused to being God-focused and prepares us as candidates for supernatural acts of God in this end time. *"If a man therefore purge himself from these, he shall be a vessel unto honour, sanctified, and meet for the master's use, and prepared unto every good work."* (2 Timothy 2:21)

A Broken and a Contrite Heart

"For thus saith the high and lofty One that inhabiteth eternity, whose name is Holy; I dwell in the high and holy place, with him also that is of a contrite and humble spirit, to revive the spirit of the humble, and to revive the heart of the contrite ones...The sacrifices of God are a broken spirit: a broken and a contrite heart, O God, thou wilt not despise...For all those things hath mine hand

made, and all those things have been, saith the Lord: but to this man will I look, even to him that is poor and of a contrite spirit, and trembleth at my word... The Lord is nigh unto them that are of a broken heart; and saveth such as be of a contrite spirit... And whosoever shall fall on this stone shall be broken: but on whomsoever it shall fall, it will grind him to powder."* (Isaiah 57:15; Psalm 51:17; Isaiah 66:2; Psalm 34:18; Jeremiah 4:3; Matthew 21:44)

Brokenness does not imply wearing a long face or harbouring a sad heart; rather, it is dying to selfism and base attitudes. Brokenness has nothing to do with thinking self-deprecating thoughts as that belittles God's creativity whose temple we are. As painful and humiliating brokenness is, it remains fundamental in paving way for God's visitation and awaited revival.

It is *"not I but Christ."* There's a difference between 'I and C'; I is bold, strong, hard, justifies self-deeds in all things and seeks its own glory outside the will of God, but C is bent, admits its wrong, gives up its right and bows to the will of God. Jesus Christ demonstrated the will of God for us by giving up everything and dying for us on the cross of Calvary. This is a place where 'I' is cancelled by a horizontal stroke. Likewise, Paul the Apostle followed Jesus' steps and gave everything up for God's glory. He declared, *"I am crucified with Christ: nevertheless I live; yet not I, but Christ liveth in me: and the life which I now live in the* flesh I live by the faith of the Son of God, who loved me, and gave himself for me." (Galatians 2:20).

Except the **SELF** is crucified, it will always be irritable, suspicious, worried, envious, resentful, critical and unyielding to God's will and purpose. SELF is the work of the flesh as enumerated in Galatians 5:19-21.

"Now the works of the flesh are manifest, which are these; dultery, fornication, uncleanness, lasciviousness, Idolatry, witchcraft, hatred, variance, emulations, wrath, strife, seditions, heresies, Envyings, murders, drunkenness, revellings, and such like: of the which I tell you before, as I have also told you in time past, that they which do such things shall not inherit the kingdom of God."

We need to break away from the works of the flesh before the fruit of the Spirit can manifest in our lives. Otherwise, any work or service rendered to God is unacceptable to God. *"So then they that are in the flesh cannot please God."* (Romans 8:8).

Anything that springs from SELF or the FLESH, however small it might look, is nothing but sin. Self-energy and self-complacency in God's service is sin.

Also, self-pity in difficult times, self-seeking in Christian work or service, self-indulgence, self-defense, self-consciousness, touchiness, hypersensitiveness, resentment, fear and worry spring from the self and defiles any man including pastors, prophets and church leaders. Evidently, revival tarries and things are not working as they should in our churches and ministries as a result of the problem of unbrokenness in us.

"Verily, verily, I say unto you, Except a corn of wheat fall into the ground and die, it abideth alone: but if it die, it bringeth forth much fruit." (John 12:24)

Brokenness is the beginning of revival. It is a sense of emptiness for God to fill us and use us for His own glory. The fact remains that the God of all creation will never use an arrogant, self-exalted and obnoxious person to compete with His glory.

Therefore, *"Sow to yourselves in righteousness, reap in mercy; break up your fallow ground: for it is time to seek the Lord, till he come and rain righteousness upon you."* (Hosea 10:12).

Broken people are self-denying and forgive easily because they know how much they have been forgiven. They are overwhelmed with a sense of their own spiritual need and esteem others better than themselves while willing to yield to the dictates of God's Spirit and to recognize their need for others.

"Let nothing be done through strife or vainglory; but in lowliness of mind let each esteem other better than themselves.... Be kindly affectioned one to another with brotherly love; in honour preferring one another;" (Philippians 2:3; Romans 12:10).

CHAPTER TWO

UPON THE MOUNT ZION

"But upon mount Zion shall be deliverance, and there shall be holiness; and the house of Jacob shall possess their possessions." (Obadiah 17)

Climbing up a mountain isn't an easy task. The nose flares and fumes as you inch up. The heart pants and body stress in labour as hot salty streams of salt break forth from body pores. But the moment you emerge on the peak in one final breathe and step, you're overwhelmed with joy that you're on top and have the vantage view of the world below. If there's any prize to claim, you've got it. Mountaineers put their lives on the line to reach the top of the world's highest mountains. They risk death not for fun but for the fame and funds.

Nobody climbs up Everest for nothing. But Mount Zion isn't a physical mound of earth and rocks. Mount Zion in the New Testament is the Church; the assembly of God's people whose Lord and Saviour is Jesus Christ. Christ rules in Zion and blesses His people in manifold ways. Deliverance, Holiness and prosperity are the sum of all real blessings any human may crave for. They are all found on Mount Zion, in the Church where Christ is Lord.

To obtain these blessings, however, you have to come out, climb up and come in. Christ's Church is up far above the rot and ruins that rule the world and seekers of Zion's blessings must step out in faith and reach out for Christ to receive.

Deliverance on Mount Zion
Sinfulness is a genetic problem. The psalmist lamented this moral depravity when he wailed, *"Behold, I was shapen in iniquity; and in sin did my mother conceive me."* (Psalm 51:5). Paul, the Apostle described his experience with sin before his conversion as that of a man sold under sin and totally powerless to free himself from the grips of iniquity.

"For the good that I would I do not: but the evil which I would not, that I do ... For I delight in the law of God after the inward man: But I see another law in my members, warring against the law of my mind, and bringing me into captivity to the law of sin which is in my members. O wretched man that I am! who shall deliver me from the body of this death? I thank God through Jesus Christ our Lord. So then with the mind I myself serve the law of God; but with the flesh the law of sin." (Romans 7:19, 22-25)

Sinfulness is not a problem anyone can solve by himself. Try as hard as you may, you can't free yourself from the grip of sin. The good news is that there's deliverance in Mount Zion the assembly of believers where Christ is Lord. Deliverance from sin is the most important blessing that Christ offers those who come to Him.

The Church doesn't set any sinner free. Christ does. Regular Church attendance and involvement in Church work don't automatically earn salvation from sin; except you meet with the Saviour, you couldn't be saved. Jesus paid the price for man's sin with His blood. He also broke the power of sin and death by His death and resurrection. Therefore, the sinner who comes to Him in repentance and faith shall be freed from the gene of sin and be saved.

Deeds of a Sinner

"Whosoever committeth sin transgresseth also the law: for sin is the transgression of the law... Now the works of the flesh are manifest, which are these; Adultery, fornication, uncleanness, lasciviousness, Idolatry, witchcraft, hatred, variance, emulations, wrath, strife, seditions, heresies, Envyings, murders, drunkenness, revellings, and such like: of the which I tell you before, as I have also told you in time past, that they which do such things shall not inherit the kingdom of God." (1 John 3:4; Galatians 5:19-21)

Sinners disobey God's commandments in thought and actions. They don't respect His laws and are always averse to His word; their understanding of the principles and practice of holy living is darkened. The devil and flesh rule the sinner's minds and dictate their actions. Sinners can't but commit sin. Although they might profess they fear and love God, their deeds pass them off as rebels.

"So they feared the Lord, and made unto themselves of the lowest of them priests of the high places, which sacrificed for them in the houses of the high places. They feared the Lord, and served their own gods, after the manner of the nations whom they carried away from thence... Having a form of godliness, but denying the power thereof: from such turn away." (2 Kings 17:32-33; 2 Timothy 3:5)

Religious hypocrisy is characteristic of sinners; self-righteousness is their means of identification, but a sinner won't inherit God's kingdom unless he/she repents and believes in Jesus.

Deliverance from Sin

"Can the Ethiopian change his skin, or the leopard his spots? then may ye also do good, that are accustomed to do evil...For I know that in me (that is, in my flesh,) dwelleth no good thing: for to will is present with me; but how to perform that which is good I find not. For the good that I would I do not: but the evil which I would not, that I do. Now if I do that I would not, it is no more I that do it, but sin that dwelleth in me. I find then a law, that, when I would do good, evil is present with me. For I delight in the law of God after the inward man: But I see another law in my members, warring against the law of my mind, and bringing me into captivity to the law of sin which is in my members. O wretched man that I am! who shall deliver me from the body of this death? I thank God through Jesus Christ our Lord. So then with the mind I myself serve the law of God; but with the flesh the law of sin... For the wages of sin is death; but the gift of God is eternal life through Jesus Christ our Lord." (Jeremiah 13:23; Romans 7:18-25; Romans 6:23)

A sinner can't deliver himself and stop sinning even if he chooses to. Salvation comes from God only through Jesus Christ. The problem of sin is more complex than any man could handle. Its power is greater than any man striving on his own can overcome; but thanks to God, the Father Who, in His love, has sent His Son to pay the price of man's salvation with His own blood and broken the power of sin by His death and resurrection. Sin and Satan were defeated by Jesus on the cross. The battle for human souls was won by Jesus then. The sin jail was broken and inmates were called out into freedom.

"Come unto me, all ye that labour and are heavy laden, and I will give you rest. Take my yoke upon you, and learn of me; for I am meek and lowly in heart: and ye shall find rest unto your souls... And you, being dead in your sins and the uncircumcision of your flesh, hath he quickened together with him, having forgiven you all trespasses; Blotting out the handwriting of ordinances that was against us, which was contrary to us, and took it out of the way, nailing it to his cross; And having spoiled principalities and powers, he made a shew of them openly, triumphing over them in it." (Matthew 11:28-29; Colossians 2:13-15)

Desire for Salvation

"Look unto me, and be ye saved, all the ends of the earth: for I am God, and there is none else... Seek ye the Lord while he may be found, call ye upon him while he is near: Let the wicked forsake his way, and the unrighteous man his thoughts: and let him return unto the Lord, and he will have mercy upon him; and to our God, for he will

abundantly pardon… For God so loved the world, that he gave his only begotten Son, that whosoever believeth in him should not perish, but have everlasting life… That if thou shalt confess with thy mouth the Lord Jesus, and shalt believe in thine heart that God hath raised him from the dead, thou shalt be saved. For with the heart man believeth unto righteousness; and with the mouth confession is made unto salvation." (Isaiah 45:22; 55:6-7; John 3:16; Romans 10:9-10)

Salvation is available free of charge by faith in Christ's death and resurrection. Yet, you wouldn't be delivered from sin if you didn't desire to be free. The table might be set and the meal arranged; but you might refuse to eat! A lot of sinners remain bound in fetters of iniquity even though the Saviour had paid the price for their release as the jail door is wide open!

To be saved, you need to:

1. Come to the Lord Jesus. *"Come unto me, all ye that labour and are heavy laden, and I will give you rest… He that believeth and is baptized shall be saved; but he that believeth not shall be damned."* (Matthew 11:28; Mark 16:16)

2. Confess your sins all of them. *"He that covereth his sins shall not prosper: but whoso confesseth and forsaketh them shall have mercy."* (Proverbs 28:13)

3. Repent of your sins. *"Then Peter said unto them,*

Repent, and be baptized every one of you in the name of Jesus Christ for the remission of sins, and ye shall receive the gift of the Holy Ghost." (Acts 2:38)

4. Correct your ways. *"That which I see not teach thou me: if I have done iniquity, I will do no more."* (Job 34:32)

5. Continue in the Lord and in fellowship. *"Then they that gladly received his word were baptized: and the same day there were added unto them about three thousand souls. And they continued stedfastly in the apostles' doctrine and fellowship, and in breaking of bread, and in prayers... And they, continuing daily with one accord in the temple, and breaking bread from house to house, did eat their meat with gladness and singleness of heart... Abide in me, and I in you. As the branch cannot bear fruit of itself, except it abide in the vine; no more can ye, except ye abide in me. I am the vine, ye are the branches: He that abideth in me, and I in him, the same bringeth forth much fruit: for without me ye can do nothing."* (Acts 2:41-42, 46; John 15:4-6). On Mount Zion, you can be delivered from sin if you would pray and believe today.

Redemptive Power in the Blood of Jesus
"For the life of the flesh is in the blood: and I have given it to you upon the altar to make an atonement for your souls: for it is the blood that maketh an atonement for the

soul... For this is my blood of the new testament, which is shed for many for the remission of sins... But with the precious blood of Christ, as of a lamb without blemish and without spot... And almost all things are by the law purged with blood; and without shedding of blood is no remission" (Leviticus 17:11; Matthew 26:28; 1 Peter 1:19; Hebrews 9:22).

The purpose of Jesus' incarnation was to shed His blood for humanity. A person obtains remission of his sins if he has faith in Christ, repents of his sins and turns away from them, then the Lord wash us from all our sins in His blood. *"...Unto him that loved us, and washed us from our sins in his own blood."* (Revelation 1:5). We have redemption, forgiveness of sins and eternal life through His own blood.

"Then Peter said unto them, Repent, and be baptized every one of you in the name of Jesus Christ for the remission of sins, and ye shall receive the gift of the Holy Ghost...Who hath delivered us from the power of darkness, and hath translated us into the kingdom of his dear Son: In whom we have redemption through his blood, even the forgiveness of sins." (Acts 2:38; Colossians 1:13-14).

The power of the blood of Jesus has provided everything we need to live a victorious life - full redemption from curses, deliverance from demons, healing of diseases, protection from evil and authority over the devil.

"Christ hath redeemed us from the curse of the law, being made a curse for us: for it is written, Cursed is every one that hangeth on a tree: That the blessing of Abraham might come on the Gentiles through Jesus Christ; that we might receive the promise of the Spirit through faith... And they overcame him by the blood of the Lamb, and by the word of their testimony; and they loved not their lives unto the death" (Acts 3:13-14; Revelation 12:11). All believers have:

1. Redemption through His blood. *"In whom we have redemption through his blood, the forgiveness of sins, according to the riches of his grace."* (Ephesians 1:7)
2. Forgiveness through His blood. (Ephesians 1:7)
3. Cleansing through His blood. *"But if we walk in the light, as he is in the light, we have fellowship one with another, and the blood of Jesus Christ his Son cleanseth us from all sin."* (I John 1:7)
4. Peace through His blood. *"And, having made peace through the blood of his cross, by him to reconcile all things unto himself; by him, I say, whether they be things in earth, or things in heaven."* (Colossians 1:20)
5. Justification through His blood. *"Much more then,*

being now justified by his blood, we shall be saved from wrath through him." (Romans 5:9)
6. Sanctification through His blood. *"By the which will we are sanctified through the offering of the body of Jesus Christ once for all."* (Hebrews 10:10)
7. We have victory through His blood. *"And they overcame him by the blood of the Lamb, and by the word of their testimony; and they loved not their lives unto the death."* (Revelation 12:11)

New Life in Christ

The greatest miracle than can ever happened to a man on earth is the miracle of salvation from sinful nature. A new life is a life that is made free from sin through Christ's sacrificial death at Calvary.

"Therefore if any man be in Christ, he is a new creature: old things are passed away; behold, all things are become new… Be ye not unequally yoked together with unbelievers: for what fellowship hath righteousness with unrighteousness? and what communion hath light with darkness? And what concord hath Christ with Belial? or what part hath he that believeth with an infidel? And what agreement huth the temple of God with idols? for ye are the temple of the living God; as God hath said, I will dwell in them, and walk in them; and I will be their God, and they shall be my people. Wherefore come out from among them, and be ye separate, saith the Lord, and

touch not the unclean thing; and I will receive you. And will be a Father unto you, and ye shall be my sons and daughters, saith the Lord Almighty... Who gave himself for us, that he might redeem us from all iniquity, and purify unto himself a peculiar people, zealous of good works." (2 Corinthians 5:17; 6:14-18; Titus 2:14).

A true Christian has believed the gospel, repented of all his sins, accepted Jesus and continues to follow Him as Lord. He lives the new life of faith and holiness and keeps his conscience void of offence towards man and God. It is a mystery. Old things are passed away and all things become new.

The new birth experience must affect our entire lifestyle and the totality of our conduct. *"And herein do I exercise myself, to have always a conscience void to offence toward God, and toward men."* (Acts 24:16). He cuts off all links that can lead him back to the old sinful habits and develops hatred for those sins which he wantonly committed before.

Having parted ways with satan, he is a new creature who, in fellowship of other Christians, serves Christ with love, humility, longsuffering, mercy, gentleness, meekness, tender-heartedness, sexual purity, discretion, sobriety, self-denial, separation, prayer, obedience to authority and such like. He leads a life that is dead to sin but alive to righteousness in Christ. *"Forasmuch as ye know that ye were not redeemed with corruptible things, as silver and gold, from your vain conversation received by tradition from your fathers; But with the precious blood of Christ, as of a lamb without blemish and without spot."* (1 Peter 1:18-19).

The new life in Christ is beautiful, refreshing, fulfilling and incomparable with anything else. It's a treasure that is more precious and greater than silver and gold. Anyone who has not tasted it should repent of their sin and be reconciled with God. In summary, a new man in Christ is:

1. Dead to sin. *"God forbid. How shall we, that are dead to sin, live any longer therein? Know ye not, that so many of us as were baptized into Jesus Christ were baptized into his death? Therefore we are buried with him by baptism into death: that like as Christ was raised up from the dead by the glory of the Father, even so we also should walk in newness of life."* (Romans 6:2-4)

2. Detached from defilement. *"Beloved, when I gave all diligence to write unto you of the common salvation, it was needful for me to write unto you, and exhort you that ye should earnestly contend for the faith which was once delivered unto the saints...Depart ye, depart ye, go ye out from thence, touch no unclean thing; go ye out of the midst of her; be ye clean, that bear the vessels of the Lord."* (Jude 3; Isaiah 52:11)

3. Dead to the world. *"Love not the world, neither the*

things that are in the world. If any man love the world, the love of the Father is not in him. For all that is in the world, the lust of the flesh, and the lust of the eyes, and the pride of life, is not of the Father, but is of the world. And the world passeth away, and the lust thereof: but he that doeth the will of God abideth for ever."* (1 John 2:15-17)

4. Crucified to the flesh. *"I am crucified with Christ: nevertheless I live; yet not I, but Christ liveth in me: and the life which I now live in the flesh I live by the faith of the Son of God, who loved me, and gave himself for me."* (Galatians 2:20)

5. Controlled by the Spirit of God. *"There is therefore now no condemnation to them which are in Christ Jesus, who walk not after the flesh, but after the Spirit... But ye are not in the flesh, but in the Spirit, if so be that the Spirit of God dwell in you. Now if any man have not the Spirit of Christ, he is none of his... But if the Spirit of him that raised up Jesus from the dead dwell in you, he that raised up Christ from the dead shall also quicken your mortal bodies by his Spirit that dwelleth in you."* (Romans 8:1, 9, 11)

6. Dutiful for the Saviour. *"Who gave himself for us, that he might redeem us from all iniquity, and purify unto himself a peculiar people, zealous of good works."* (Titus 2:14)

7. An enemy to satan. *"We know that whosoever is born of God sinneth not; but he that is begotten of God keepeth himself, and that wicked one toucheth him not."* (1 John 5:18)

8. Baptized by immersion: *"And Jesus came and spake unto them, saying, All power is given unto me in heaven and in earth. Go ye therefore, and teach all nations, baptizing them in the name of the Father, and of the Son, and of the Holy Ghost: Teaching them to observe all things whatsoever I have commanded you: and, lo, I am with you always, even unto the end of the world. Amen...And he said unto them, Go ye into all the world, and preach the gospel to every creature. He that believeth and is baptized shall be saved; but he that believeth not shall be damned...Then Peter said unto them, Repent, and be baptized every one of you in the name of Jesus Christ for the remission of sins, and ye shall receive the gift of the Holy Ghost"* (Matthew 28:18-20; Mark 16:15-16; Acts 2:38).

Our Lord Jesus commanded that those who believe should be baptized and it is the expected norm for believers in the New Testament to do so. The word *baptize* means to dip or immerse, not sprinkle water or used as the sign of the cross on the forehead. Water baptism is public identification of saved believer with Christ in His death and resurrection. A baptized believer publicly declares that he is a new person in Christ and now belongs to the body of Christ. *"Know ye not, that so many of us as were baptized into Jesus Christ were baptized into his death? Therefore we are buried with him by baptism into death: that like as Christ was raised up from the dead by the glory of the Father, even so we also should walk in newness of life. For if we have been planted together in the likeness of his death, we shall be also in the likeness of his resurrection."* (Romans 6:3-5). It is important to know that Water Baptism is one immersion (not three) "In the name of the Father, and of the Son, and of the Holy Ghost" as Jesus commanded, so we must obey. Only those who have repented of their sins, accepted Jesus Christ as their Lord and Saviour and decided to follow Him are qualified for water baptism by immersion.

Caution Against the Old Lifestyle

"Let not sin therefore reign in your mortal body, that ye should obey it in the lusts thereof. Neither yield ye your members as instruments of unrighteousness unto sin: but yield yourselves unto God, as those that are alive from the dead, and your members as instruments of righteousness unto God. For sin shall not have dominion over you: for ye are not under the law, but under grace... My son, if sinners entice thee, consent thou not...For if after they have escaped the pollutions of the world

through the knowledge of the Lord and Saviour Jesus Christ, they are again entangled therein, and overcome, the latter end is worse with them than the beginning. For it had been better for them not to have known the way of righteousness, than, after they have known it, to turn from the holy commandment delivered unto them. But it is happened unto them according to the true proverb, The dog is turned to his own vomit again; and the sow that was washed to her wallowing in the mire" (Romans 6:12-14; Proverbs 1:10; 2 Peter 2:20-22).

Being a Bible Christian doesn't insulate the believer against backsliding. The devil isn't far away; he tempted our Lord Jesus Christ in His earthly ministry. Sin would loom into view from time to time. The old lifestyle beckons the Christians regardless of the level of spiritual perfection he has attained. Therefore, the Bible contains warnings against the danger of relapsing into the old way of living. The summary of the warnings is that the Christian should resist wrong promptings, reject canal offers, restrain his body, bounce back with prayers and remain in the grace of the Lord.

"Looking diligently lest any man fail of the grace of God; lest any rool of bitterness springing up trouble you, and thereby many be defiled; Lest there be any fornicator, or profane person, as Esau, who for one morsel of meat sold his birthright. For ye know how that afterward, when he would have inherited the blessing, he was rejected: for he

found no place of repentance, though he sought it carefully with tears." (Hebrews 12:15-17)

Clean Hands and a Pure Heart

"Who shall ascend into the hill of the Lord? or who shall stand in his holy place? He that hath clean hands, and a pure heart; who hath not lifted up his soul unto vanity, nor sworn deceitfully... Lord, who shall abide in thy tabernacle? who shall dwell in thy holy hill? He that walketh uprightly, and worketh righteousness, and speaketh the truth in his heart. He that backbiteth not with his tongue, nor doeth evil to his neighbour, nor taketh up a reproach against his neighbour. In whose eyes a vile person is contemned; but he honoureth them that fear the Lord. He that sweareth to his own hurt, and changeth not. He that putteth not out his money to usury, nor taketh reward against the innocent. He that doeth these things shall never be moved." (Psalm 24:3-4; 15:1-5).

David, a man of God's heart, asked a question regarding the qualifications for standing in God's presence. The answers to his request came to him from God that 'he that has **clean hands** and **a pure heart**.' It's not either of the two, but both are required to see God. This simply implies holiness within and holiness without, that is, holiness in its entirety, the call of God on all men and women. *"Follow peace with all men, and holiness, without which no man shall see the Lord."* (Hebrews 12:14). '**Clean hands in the old**

testament and following peace with all men in the new testament ...' are closely related because both refer to our spiritual condition that people can easily see.

In other words, it connotes the salvation experience and deliverance from the outward sins we committed against ourselves and fellow human beings. It is a new life from God through Christ with power over outward sins of every kind. The book of Galatians 5:19-21 and 1 Corinthians 6:9-11 enumerated the works of the flesh (outward sins) to us: "*Now the works of the flesh are manifest, which are these; Adultery, fornication, uncleanness, lasciviousness, Idolatry, witchcraft, hatred, variance, emulations, wrath, strife, seditions, heresies, Envyings, murders, drunkenness, revellings, and such like: of the which I tell you before, as I have also told you in time past, that they which do such things shall not inherit the kingdom of God...Know ye not that the unrighteous shall not inherit the kingdom of God? Be not deceived: neither fornicators, nor idolaters, nor adulterers, nor effeminate, nor abusers of themselves with mankind, Nor thieves, nor covetous, nor drunkards, nor revilers, nor extortioners, shall inherit the kingdom of God.*"

Thank God for the Blood of Jesus Christ that cleanses us from all sins. The evidence of our salvation in Christ is that old thing are passed away. Your language, appearance and dressing will be new when you in are Christ.

At this point, we are not looking at others as our models; Christ is our perfect Model and Standard of lifestyle and living. Therefore, we are looking unto Christ, the Author and Finisher of our faith. We experience a desire to love and follow Christ in all things with the joy of salvation in our new birth. Whereas, a pure heart and holiness mean the same thing. The heart is a hidden thing, it's an inward thing we do not see, only God Himself sees and knows every thought going on inside of us. In Jeremiah 17: 9-10 says, *"The heart is deceitful above all things, and desperately wicked: who can know it? I the Lord search the heart, I try the reins, even to give every man according to his ways, and according to the fruit of his doings."*

The natural heart of man is a generating engine of thoughts. The thought of doing evil to our fellow man originated from the heart. When you cut a tree, there's tendency for it to grow out shoots again, but when you destroy the roots, you destroy the tree altogether. There are those who demonstrate clean hands, manifesting a kind of outward holiness in their public life but whose hearts are full of envy, hatred, bitterness, evil thoughts, selfish motives, to mention a few.

Likewise, there are people who claim that their hearts are pure even when their visible lives are devoid of godly virtues of love, meekness, kindness, gentleness, longsuffering, temperance, peace, joy and faith. This is the reason Paul the Apostle, by inspiration, admonished us in 2 Corinthians 7:1, *"Having therefore these promises, dearly beloved, let us cleanse ourselves from all filthiness of the flesh and spirit, perfecting holiness in the fear of God."* When a child is born, he doesn't remain a perpetual babe. He has to grow.

Therefore, we must perfect the holiness gotten at salvation in pure heart (holiness or sanctification). This is the seconded work of grace needed for seeing God. Clean hands or Salvation represents our passport needed for our journey to see God. Pure heart is our qualifying visa to see God. In Leviticus 20:8, *"And ye shall keep my statutes, and do them: I am the LORD which sanctify you."*

Jesus Christ our Lord and Saviour prayed for the sanctification of his followers in the book of John 17:17, *"Sanctify them through thy truth: thy word is truth."* God is the one that sanctifies His people (not sinners).

It's possible to be sanctified, so, we should go beyond mental knowledge and get the experience through prayers. Therefore, *"Abstain from all appearance of evil. And the very God of peace sanctify you wholly; and I pray God your whole spirit and soul and body be preserved blameless unto the coming of our Lord Jesus Christ. Faithful is he that calleth you, who also will do it."* The need for the Christian worker to stand right before God and man makes sanctification or holiness (holy living) imperative in the lives of heaven-bound Christians. The necessity of continuous anointing demands holy living. Sanctification is non-negotiable to a Christian leader who wants to be "... *a vessel unto honour, sanctified, and meet for the master's use, and prepared unto every good work.*" (2 Timothy 2:21)

CHAPTER THREE

OUR DAILY BREAD

"Then said the Lord unto Moses, Behold, I will rain bread from heaven for you; and the people shall go out and gather a certain rate every day, that I may prove them, whether they will walk in my law, or no... And when the children of Israel saw it, they said one to another, It is manna: for they wist not what it was. And Moses said unto them, This is the bread which the Lord hath given you to eat... Be not carried about with divers and strange doctrines. For it is a good thing that the heart be established with grace; not with meats, which have not profited them that have been occupied therein... That we henceforth be no more children, tossed to and fro, and carried about with every wind of doctrine, by the sleight of men, and cunning craftiness, whereby they lie in wait

to deceive" (Exodus 16:4, 15; Hebrews 13:9; Ephesians 4:14).

Man needs bread to live. Nevertheless, *"Man shall not live by bread alone but, by every word that proceedeth out of the mouth of God."* (Mathew 4:4). Truly, the word of God and the strength we derive from it is more important than our daily meal. So, God's word really is what we need for spiritual growth and stability.

"Then said the Lord unto Moses, behold I will rain bread from heaven ... and the people shall ... gather certain rate every day ... and when the children of Israel saw it, they said ... it is manna ... and Moses said unto them, this is the bread which the Lord hath given you to eat." (Exodus 16:4, 15)

As God expected the children of Israelites to gather each day a portion of manna that was just enough for one day, Christians (who are spiritual Israelites) must form the rewarding habit of gathering daily a portion of the soul's spiritual food. Daily reading of the Scriptures is central to our lives for a number of reasons.

1. The Bible nourishes us and keeps us alive. "*...Man doth not live by bread only, but by every word that proceedeth*

out of the mouth of the Lord doth man live." (Deuteronomy 8:3)

2. The Bible teaches us the fear of God, which prolongs life (Proverbs 10:27); "...*forget not my law; but let thine heart keep my commandments: For length of days, and long life, and peace, shall they add to thee.*" (Proverbs 3:1-2)

3. The Bible guides and directs us: "*Thy word is a lamp unto my feet, and a light unto my path.*" (Psalm 119:105)

4. The Bible shows us our true spiritual state and the way out of such deplorable state. According to Job, "*I have heard of thee by the hearing of the ear ... wherefore I abhor myself and repent in dust and ashes.*" (Job 42:5-6)

5. The Bible gives us victory by producing faith in us. (Romans 10:17) "*... and this is the victory that overcometh the world, even our faith.*" (1 John 5:4)

6. The Bible is our standard for making decisions, forming opinions and establishing doctrines in every area of life. (1 Timothy 3:16-17; 2 Timothy 3:16)

7. The Bible gives us joy and comfort in spite of life's inevitable tempest, tumults and troubles. (Psalm 34:19)

8. The Bible teaches us right relationships between us and our fellows, always bringing the golden rule to the fore. (Matthew 7:12)

9. The Bible gives us the hope of eternal life: *"Search the scriptures; for in them ye think ye have eternal life: and they are they which testify of me."* (John 5:39)

10. With the scriptural knowledge of the resurrection of the dead (1Corinthians 15:55) and the translation of the saints, the believer sees the light at the end of the tunnel. The portals of death are no longer cheerless.

In this world, do you know that you are the salt of the earth? Is there an aura of sweetness around you as a Christian? Is there still smiles on your face or you scare others from yourself and from the Kingdom of God? How about righteous living? You are the salt of the earth but, *"If the salt have lost his savour, wherewith shall it be seasoned? It is henceforth good for nothing."* (Luke 14:34; Matthew 5:13).

Remember that you are to read your Bible every day, prayerfully, devotionally and meditatively. *"Man shall not live by bread alone; but by every word that proceedeth out of the mouth of God."* (Matthew 4:4)

The word 'Bible'

The word Bible means the Book. The name shows the degree of its importance beyond any other book. The Bible is worth being named as if there were no other books at all because it is the Book of books and arguably the first book printed on an industrial printing machine in the 15th century by John Gutenberg. The word is Greek and when first usedused, it was in plural. Biblia or "the books" (extracted from *Hitchcock's New and Complete Analysis of the Holy Bible).*

Names and Titles of the Bible

The Bible is referred as:

The Scriptures says in 2 Timothy 3:16-17, "*All scripture is given by inspiration of God, and is profitable for doctrine, for reproof, for correction, for instruction in righteousness: That the man of God may be perfect, thoroughly furnished unto all good works.*" (Read John 7:38)

The Scriptures: In John 5:39, "*Search the scriptures; for in them ye think ye have eternal life: and they are they which testify of me.*" (Read Luke 24:27; Acts 17:11)

The Holy Scriptures: In the book of 2 Timothy 3:15 "*And that from a child thou hast known the holy scriptures, which are able to make thee wise unto salvation through faith which is in Christ Jesus."* (Read Romans 1:2)

The Oracles of God: In Hebrews 5:12, *"For when for the time ye ought to be teachers, ye have need that one teach you again which be the first principles of the oracles of God; and are become such as have need of milk, and not of strong meat."* (Read Romans 3:2)

The Book of the Lord: In the Book of Isaiah 34:16, *"Seek ye out of the book of the Lord, and read: no one of these shall fail, none shall want her mate: for my mouth it hath commanded, and his spirit it hath gathered them."*

The Word of God: The book of Hebrews 4:12 says, *"For the word of God is quick, and powerful, and sharper than any twoedged sword, piercing even to the dividing asunder of soul and spirit, and of the joints and marrow, and is a discerner of the thoughts and intents of the heart."* (Read Mark 7:13; Romans 10:17)

The Sword of the Spirit: Ephesians 6:17 says, *"And take the helmet of salvation, and the sword of the Spirit, which is the word of God."*

The Old and New Testament: The book of Hebrews 9:15 says, *"And for this cause he is the mediator of the new testament, that by means of death, for the redemption of the transgressions that were under the first testament, they which are called might receive the promise of eternal inheritance."* (Read Luke 22:20; 2 Corinthians 3:6-15)

The Word of Christ: Colossians 3:16 says, *"Let the word of Christ dwell in you richly in all wisdom; teaching and admonishing one another in psalms and hymns and spiritual songs, singing with grace in your hearts to the Lord."*

The Word of Life: In Philippians 2:16, the Bible says, *"Holding forth the word of life; that I may rejoice in the day of Christ, that I have not run in vain, neither laboured in vain."*

The Scripture of Truth: Daniel 10:21 says, *"But I will shew thee that which is noted in the scripture of truth: and there is none that holdeth with me in these things, but Michael your prince."*

The Word of Truth: 2 Timothy 2:15 stated, *"Study to shew thyself approved unto God, a workman that needeth not to be ashamed, rightly dividing the word of truth."*

The Symbols of the Bible

Mirror: *"For if any be a hearer of the word, and not a doer, he is like unto a man beholding his natural face in a glass: For he beholdeth himself, and goeth his way, and straightway forgetteth what manner of man he was. But whoso looketh into the perfect law of liberty, and continueth therein, he being not a forgetful hearer, but a doer of the work, this man shall be blessed in his deed"* (James 1:23-25). It is called mirror because it reflects the mind of God and the rue condition of man.

A Seed: "*Now the parable is this: The seed is the word of God.. Being born again, not of corruptible seed, but of incorruptible, by the word of God, which liveth and abideth forever*" (Luke 8:11; 1 Peter 1:23). It is called seed because, once properly planted, it brings forth life, growth and fruit.

Water: "*Husbands, love your wives, even as Christ also loved the church, and gave himself for it; That he might sanctify and cleanse it with the washing of water by the word, That he might present it to himself a glorious church, not having spot, or wrinkle, or any such thing; but that it should be holy and without blemish*" (Ephesians 5:25-27. Read Isaiah 55:10). It is called water because of its cleansing, quenching and refreshing qualities.

A Lamp: "*Thy word is a lamp unto my feet, and a light unto my path... We have also a more sure word of prophecy; whereunto ye do well that ye take heed, as unto a light that shineth in a dark place, until the day dawn, and the day star arise in your hearts*" (Psalms 119:105; 2 Peter 1:19; and read Proverbs 6:23). It is called a Lamp because it shows us where we are now, it guides us in the next step and it keeps us from falling.

A Sword: "*For the word of God is quick, and powerful, and sharper than any twoedged sword, piercing even to the dividing asunder of soul and spirit, and of the joints* and marrow, and is a discerner of the thoughts and intents of the heart... And take the helmet of salvation, and the sword of the Spirit, which is the word of God"* (Hebrews 4:12; Ephesians 6:17). It is called Sword because of its piercing ability, operating with equal effectiveness upon sinners, saints and satan and his cohorts.

Milk, Meat, Bread and Honey: *"As newborn babes, desire the sincere milk of the word, that ye may grow thereby... For when for the time ye ought to be teachers, ye have need that one teach you again which be the first principles of the oracles of God; and are become such as have need of milk, and not of strong meat. For every one that useth milk is unskilful in the word of righteousness: for he is a babe. But strong meat belongeth to them that are of full age, even those who by reason of use have their senses exercised to discern both good and evil... I am the living bread which came down from heaven: if any man eat of this bread, he shall live for ever: and the bread that I will give is my flesh, which I will give for the life of the world... More to be desired are they than gold, yea, than much fine gold: sweeter also than honey and the honeycomb"* (1 Peter 2:2; Hebrews 5:12-14; John 6:51; Psalms 19:10). It is referred to as nourishing food because of the strength it imparts.

Hammer: *"Is not my word like as a fire? saith the Lord; and like a hammer that breaketh the rock in pieces?"* (Jeremiah 23:29). It has the ability both to tear down and to build up.

Fire: *"And they said one to another, Did not our heart burn within us, while he talked with us by the way, and while he opened to us the scriptures?... Then I said, I will not make mention of him, nor speak any more in his name. But his word was in mine heart as a burning fire shut up in my bones, and I was weary with forbearing, and I could not stay"* (Luke 24:32; Jeremiah 20:9). It is called fire because of its judging, purifying and consuming abilities.

CHAPTER FOUR

PERSECUTION AND TEMPTATION

"And Saul was consenting unto his death. And at that time there was a great persecution against the church which was at Jerusalem; and they were all scattered abroad throughout the regions of Judaea and Samaria, except the apostles. And devout men carried Stephen to his burial, and made great lamentation over him. As for Saul, he made havock of the church, entering into every house, and haling men and women committed them to prison. Therefore they that were scattered abroad went everywhere preaching the word ... For we have not an high priest which cannot be touched with the feeling of our infirmities; but was in all points tempted like as we are, yet without sin." (Acts 8:1-4; Hebrews 4:15)

Both Persecution and Temptation are common to all Christians without exception. They are necessary hurdles to scale over before winning the prize. The reason satan uses these tools against us is to derail our Christian journey to life eternal. People may call you different names such as old-fashioned Christian or accuse you wrongly with a threat to kill you. Likewise, persecutors may tempt you to do something contrary to God's will and standard or you may get strongly tempted of your own lust at a time of your weakness.

In any situation, remember that you're not alone in your journey, the Captain of our salvation is always there and understands what you are passing through or when the billows roll and He intercedes for us from time to time. *"Who shall separate us from the love of Christ? shall tribulation, or distress, or persecution, or famine, or nakedness, or peril, or sword? As it is written, for thy sake we are killed all the day long; we are accounted as sheep for the slaughter. Nay, in all these things we are more than conquerors through him that loved us"* (Romans 8:35-37). By His grace, we shall not fall but sail through make it in the mighty name of Jesus Christ!

Persecution is Certain
Persecution means the suffering of Christians for their faith in Christ Jesus. Our Lord and Saviour did not hide

Persecution and Temptation

this salient truth from us in His earthly ministry. In the book of Matthew 5:10-12, He says, *"Blessed are they which are persecuted for righteousness' sake: for theirs is the kingdom of heaven. Blessed are ye, when men shall revile you, and persecute you, and shall say all manner of evil against you falsely, for my sake. Rejoice, and be exceeding glad: for great is your reward in heaven: for so persecuted they the prophets which were before you."*

Persecutions are the common experience of all believers. When it first appeared in the family of Adam, Cain slew Abel. Why? Because his own works were evil and his brother's righteous (1 John 3:12). When it appeared in the family of Abraham, Ishmael, who was born after the flesh, persecuted Isaac, who was born after the spirit (Galatians 4:29).

Joseph was hated and sold into slavery by his brethren for relating his God-given dreams. Moses was derided by some rebel leaders as he led Israel under God's guidance through the wilderness. David was greatly persecuted by King Saul. Isaiah was cut into two with carpenter's iron saw. Jeremiah, Elijah, Elisha and other prophets suffered for upholding the scepter of righteousness as did Shadrack, Meshack, Abednego and Daniel for taking their stand in worshipping the only true God. The Lord Jesus Christ was vehemently persecuted by the religionists of His day. Who could have thought that Jesus would be persecuted in spite of what he did for humanity!

The early church leaders (and members) suffered persecution in the hands of religious Jews as well as pagan Gentiles wherever they preached the gospel. They were arrested, whipped, jailed and sometimes, martyred for speaking in the name of the Lord Jesus. Persecution often comes from those who disagree with God's plan.

"For ye, brethren, became followers of the churches of God which in Judaea are in Christ Jesus: for ye also have suffered like things of your own countrymen, even as they have of the Jews: Who both killed the Lord Jesus, and their own prophets, and have persecuted us; and they please not God, and are contrary to all men: Forbidding us to speak to the Gentiles that they might be saved, to fill up their sins alway: for the wrath is come upon them to the uttermost." (1Thessalonians 2:14-16)

It comes from the children of the devil and sometimes from believers who allow themselves to be used by the devil. Persecution may take various forms such as slanders, hatred, reviling, abuses, insult, having one's promotion withheld or one's entitlements seized by one's parents, being denied jobs that one is qualified for as a result of your colour or race. "*Yea, and all that will live godly in Christ Jesus shall suffer persecution*" (2 Timothy 3:12). Since persecution is sure and certain, every believer must maintain their love, peace, joy and faith during persecution and be ever conscious of the eternal weight of glory that awaits him in heaven.

"I know thy works, and tribulation, and poverty, (but thou art rich) and I know the blasphemy of them which say they are Jews, and are not, but are the synagogue of Satan. Fear none of those things which thou shalt suffer: behold, the devil shall cast some of you into prison, that ye may be tried; and ye shall have tribulation ten days: be thou faithful unto death, and I will give thee a crown of life... He that overcometh shall inherit all things; and I will be his God, and he shall be my son." (Revelation 2:9-10; 21:7)

Holding on to our integrity and faith will bring the victory with great heavenly reward for us as we endure to the end. "*And ye shall be hated of all men for my name's sake: but he that endureth to the end shall be saved.*" (Matthew 10:22)

Temptation is Sure

"*Blessed is the man that endureth temptation: for when he is tried, he shall receive the crown of life, which the*

Lord hath promised to them that love him. Let no man say when he is tempted, I am tempted of God: for God cannot be tempted with evil, neither tempteth he any man: But every man is tempted, when he is drawn away of his own lust, and enticed. Then when lust hath conceived, it bringeth forth sin: and sin, when it is finished, bringeth forth death" (James 1:12-15).

Temptation itself is not sinning until you are drawn away and yield to it. It is common knowledge that we cannot keep the birds of the air from flying over our head, but we can keep them from building a nest in our hair. So is temptation. It is a universal experience of all children of God. It can come in form an enticement, a thought or a suggestion to sin or do evil.

Temptation is a leveller; it cuts across all ages, races, colours, ranks, social classes, spiritual levels or estates in life even in the Bible days. No saint has lived long enough or grown old enough in grace as to not get tempted from time to time or get rid of it.

The tempter is the devil and his agents (spirits and human beings). His target is to bring a stumbling block (temptation) in the pathway of Christians. *"There hath no temptation taken you but such as is common to man: but God is faithful, who will not suffer you to be tempted above that ye are able; but will with the temptation also make a way to escape, that ye may be able to bear it."* (1Corinthians 10:13)

God is never the author of temptation to sin. Why then does God permit temptation? God permits temptation as a trial for the perfecting of the Christian's spiritual motive but He is neither the immediate nor the remote cause of it. God limits satan in the temptations he thrusts at His faithful children.

Temptation begins with man's desire which may be perfectly legitimate in itself but which goes astray, thus leading men away from his God to a baser, inferior and transient ideal. The greatest source of temptation is the heart hosting the enemy within such as pride, lust, revenge and envy. The Bible says, *"Keep thy heart with all diligence; for out of it are the issues of life"* (Proverbs 4:23). In the New Testament, Christ says, *"For from within, out of the heart of men, proceed evil thoughts, adulteries, fornications, murders, thefts, covetousness, an evil eye, blasphemy, pride, foolishness: All these evil things come from within and defile the man"* (Mark 7:21-23).

Neighbours, relations or even parents can be sources of temptation. They can impress unscriptural ideals, practices and sentiments on our minds and evoke the base nature in us. Another source of temptation is the flesh. The inordinate cravings of the flesh in the areas of appetite and immorality urge and lead men into temptation. The believer's weakest point or his besetting sin is a sure spot or source of temptation. *"Wherefore seeing we also are compassed about with so great a cloud of witnesses, let us lay aside every weight, and the sin which doth so easily beset us, and let us run with patience the race that is set before us"* (Hebrews 12:1).

Overconfidence, closeness between opposite sexes and the crazy get-rich-quick syndrome are sources of temptation believers must avoid. To overcome, there must be strong passion for Christ - to do His will, to keep our living relationship with the Lord intact and to always exalt and honour Christ in word and deed. Joseph overcame in Potiphar's house and we can overcome by His grace. Gold must be refined; so, the Christian's character must be developed and strengthened to crush temptation consistently.

CHAPTER FIVE

THE FRUIT OF THE SPIRIT

But the fruit of the Spirit is love, joy, peace, longsuffering, gentleness, goodness, faith, meekness, temperance: against such there is no law." (Galatians 5:22, 23)

Wherefore by their fruits ye shall know them... (for the fruit of the Light consists in all goodness and righteousness and truth)" (Matthew 7:20; Ephesians 5:9)

The fruit of the Spirit represents the visible marks of Christ's life; it is Christ reproduced in the believer who has given his life to the Lord. As the branch (believers) abides in the True Vine (Jesus Christ), believers are expected to bear fruit as mentioned above. *"I am the true vine, and my Father is the husbandman. Every branch in me that beareth not fruit he taketh away: and every branch that beareth fruit, he purgeth it, that it may bring forth more fruit."* (John 15:1-2). Anywhere the fruit of the Spirit is found, it is clear that there is the new birth because these marks cannot be produced by the human spirit or human efforts.

Everyone that is born again should bear the fruit of the Spirit. To remain fruitful, we must abide firmly in Christ by obeying His word. Then, the character of Christ can be reproduced in our lives through the Holy Spirit and Christ's identity mark imprinted in us as His true disciples. *"If ye abide in me, and my words abide in you, ye shall ask what ye will, and it shall be done unto you. Herein is my Father glorified, that ye bear much fruit; so shall ye be my disciples."* (John 15:7-8).

There are nine characters of the fruit produced by the Spirit. The singular term "fruit" means they are to function together. Love is the basic essential life of Christ; it embraces all the other attributes.

Love
Love is all-encompassing as a divine attribute of God that surpasses human understanding. It fills a person with the fullness of God by the power of the Holy Spirit. This love is not lusting or carnal attitude. It's sacrificial in nature as

the essence of Christ's death for us on the cross. *"For God so loved the world, that he gave his only begotten Son, that whosoever believeth in him should not perish, but have everlasting life."* (John 3:16). Other characters of love can be found in the book of 1 Corinthians 13:4-8; *"Charity (love) suffereth long, and is kind; charity envieth not; charity vaunteth not itself, is not puffed up, Doth not behave itself unseemly, seeketh not her own, is not easily provoked, thinketh no evil; Rejoiceth not in iniquity, but rejoiceth in the truth; Beareth all things, believeth all things, hopeth all things, endureth all things. Charity never faileth: but whether there be prophecies, they shall fail; whether there be tongues, they shall cease; whether there be knowledge, it shall vanish away."*

Therefore, whosoever has this attribute has fulfilled the law and whosoever lives in love lives in God and God in him. However, it must be reiterated that God is love but love is not God.

Joy

Joy is not happiness, it's God-given. Happiness is based on happenings and it's ephemeral and flickers in the tide of events. *"For the kingdom of God is not meat and drink; but righteousness, and peace, and joy in the Holy Ghost"* (Romans 14:17). Joy gives spiritual strength to every believer in Christ Jesus and true joy comes from believer's salvation. It is the result of our right relationship with God in any situation we find ourselves whether sweet or bitter, good or bad, pleasant or unpleasant, painful or pleasurable; our joy is not affected or diminished, it remains constant. Joy is greater than the greatest of all happiness. It is the source of the greatest strength of the believer. *"Then he said unto them, Go your way, eat the fat, and drink the sweet, and send portions unto them for whom nothing is prepared: for this day is holy unto our Lord: neither be ye sorry; for the joy of the Lord is your strength."* (Nehemiah 8:10)

Peace
This fruit of Holy Spirit grants us peace with God, our fellowmen and ourselves. The spiritual fruit of peace results from being justified by faith. In Romans 5:1 and Hebrews 12:14, *"Therefore being justified by faith, we have peace with God through our Lord Jesus Christ… Follow peace with all men, and holiness, without which no man shall see the Lord."* True peace is the absence of enmity between man and God. It's having a good relationship with God and harmony with ourselves even in persecution. It implies friendliness with one another, having a stable emotion and contentment in whatever condition. Divine peace keeps us calm in a boisterous circumstance and within the limits of God's will even in the storms of life.

Longsuffering
Longsuffering can be defined as endurance without complaining. It entails carrying the cross without

necessarily seeking relief. A believer who has this quality does not ask for a lighter load but for a stronger back. This is love on trial that enables you to be emotionally strong and forgive others easily. It's explicit in Revelation 2:10, *"Fear none of those things which thou shalt suffer: behold, the devil shall cast some of you into prison, that ye may be tried; and ye shall have tribulation ten days: be thou faithful unto death, and I will give thee a crown of life."* Paul enjoined saints in Colossians 3:12-13, *"Put on therefore, as the elect of God, holy and beloved, bowels of mercies, kindness, humbleness of mind, meekness, longsuffering; Forbearing one another, and forgiving one another, if any man have a quarrel against any: even as Christ forgave you, so also do ye."*

Gentleness
Gentleness is the inner quality of heart attitude that manifests the true nature of Christ in a transformed believer. *"But let it be the hidden man of the heart, in that which is not corruptible, even the ornament of a meek and quiet spirit, which is in the sight of God of great price."* (1 Peter 3:4). It is an act of grace to accept correction without disputing and to submit without concern for one's own rights. In 2 Timothy 2:24; *"And the servant of the Lord must not strive; but be gentle unto all men, apt to teach, patient."*

Goodness
Goodness is synonymous with kindness. It is the act of

doing the right thing for the right reason by the grace of God. Goodness enables you to do good to those who hate you as well as those of the household of faith. *"For we are his workmanship, created in Christ Jesus unto good works, which God hath before ordained that we should walk in them"* (Ephesians 2:10). It is a benign attitude towards others without discrimination. *"But I say unto you which hear, Love your enemies, do good to them which hate you… As we have therefore opportunity, let us do good unto all men, especially unto them who are of the household of faith."* (Luke 6:27; Galatians 6:10)

Faith
Faith is trusting God in all situations and more especially for the impossible. It is an assurance of expectations and an evidence of the invisible as opposed to reason or logic. It's sublime yet without faith, no one can please God. *"Now faith is the substance of things hoped for, the evidence of things not seen… But without faith it is impossible to please him: for he that cometh to God must believe that he is, and that he is a rewarder of them that diligently seek him"* (Hebrews 11:1, 6).

Faith is the first ingredient in the equation of salvation that provokes genuine repentance. *"For by grace are ye saved through faith; and that not of yourselves: it is the gift of God:"… They that trust in the Lord shall be as mount Zion, which cannot be removed, but abideth for ever"* (Ephesians

2:8; Psalms 125:1). It's a reliance on God's Omniscience, Omnipotence and Omnipresence. Faith does not take no for an answer but it very actively presses on even where there have been disappointments. Faith is being incurably optimistic with divine backing and taking calculated risks.

Meekness

Meekness is the highest degree of gentleness that feels not jealous nor envious but patient and sustaining servant-like submission to God in all things. *"Blessed are the meek: for they shall inherit the earth"* (Matthew 5:5). The meek would not make haste to violently struggle for anything, however precious; not even for their own rights when it is at crossroads with others'. They don't engage in competition and show-offs. Meekness is being gentle, pliant, flexible but firm and frank. *"But the meek shall inherit the earth; and shall delight themselves in the abundance of peace."* (Psalms 37:11)

Temperance

Temperance or Self-control is abstinence from all that is evil and moderate use of all that is good. It can be construed as a high sense of personal discipline that shuns excesses and cautions against superfluity.

"And every man that striveth for the mastery is temperate in all things. Now they do it to obtain a

corruptible crown; but we an incorruptible... Wherefore lay apart all filthiness and superfluity of naughtiness, and receive with meekness the engrafted word, which is able to save your souls (1 Corinthians 9:25; James 1:21).

Temperate or self-controlled persons hate waste and are meticulous and careful with their resources. They are not frivolous and so, hardly ever get into trouble. Such people don't break traffic rules or other regulations even when no one was watching. They also don't get easily carried away by glitters that sway the carefree.

CHAPTER SIX

TRUE DISCIPLESHIP

"Then said Jesus unto his disciples, If any man will come after me, let him deny himself, and take up his cross, and follow me...Then said Jesus to those Jews which believed on him, If ye continue in my word, then are ye my disciples indeed; And ye shall know the truth, and the truth shall make you free...For even hereunto were ye called: because Christ also suffered for us, leaving us an example, that ye should follow his steps: Who did no sin, neither was guile found in his mouth: Who, when he was reviled, reviled not again; when he suffered, he threatened not; but committed himself to him that judgeth righteously" (Matthew 16:24; John 8:31-32; 1 Peter 2:21-23).

True discipleship is being a disciple of the Lord Jesus Christ. The true disciple of Christ belongs to a social unique class of people. They are 'different from the rest of the people.' The process of discipleship begins at regeneration, when the person comes to Christ in repentance and faith in Christ. No one becomes a disciple by self-righteousness, the best of which is like filthy rags.

A true disciple is one who has received pardon, peace and the grace of God; he denies himself and then begins to follow Christ. The love of sin, carnal comparisons, unedifying words, carnal principles and selfish ambition are non-existent in his life any more. *"And whosoever doth not bear his cross, and come after me, cannot be my disciple."* (Luke 14:27; Also, read Romans 15:1-3)

Although the cross may be heavy, shameful and intolerable to the flesh, the disciple endures it without complaining. He has received the grace to forsake all things. *"Then answered Peter and said unto him, Behold, we have forsaken all, and followed thee; what shall we have therefore?... And every one that hath forsaken houses, or brethren, or sisters, or father, or mother, or wife, or children, or lands, for my name's sake, shall receive an hundredfold, and shall inherit everlasting life"* (Matthew 19:27, 29).

The disciple's love for Christ and the brethren is real, harmless and unselfish, not according to the wisdom of men. *"For he whom God hath sent speaketh the words of God: for God giveth not the Spirit by measure unto him. The Father loveth the Son, and hath given all things into his hand"* (John 3:34-35). He has pledged his complete obedience to God's unchanging word and will never go back whatever worldly attraction or temptation may come his way. *"In whose eyes a vile person is contemned; but he honoureth them that fear the Lord. He that sweareth to his own hurt, and changeth not"* (Psalms 15:4). Many are disciples of men, but only few are true disciples of Christ.

The Call to Christian Discipleship: *"And he saith unto them, Follow me, and I will make you fishers of men. And they straightway left their nets, and followed him. And going on from thence, he saw other two brethren, James the son of Zebedee, and John his brother, in a ship with Zebedee their father, mending their nets; and he called them. And they immediately left the ship and their father, and followed him… For even hereunto were ye called: because Christ also suffered for us, leaving us an example, that ye should follow his steps:"* (Matthew 4:19-22; 1 Peter 2:21). All through His ministry, our Lord Jesus had always called people to follow Him in lifestyle and practices and not to just be ordinary escorts or protocols.

Today, much church leadership failed to realize that Jesus has not sent the church to be making denominational church-members but disciples all over the world. Jesus said in Matthew 28:19-20, *"Go ye therefore, and teach all* nations, baptizing them in the name of the Father, and of the Son, and of the Holy Ghost: Teaching them to observe all things whatsoever I have commanded you: and, lo, I am with you alway, even unto the end of the world. Amen." (Read Matthew 9:9; Mark 10:17-21; Luke 9:57-59; John 1:43)

Definition of Christian Discipleship: *"Take my yoke upon you, and learn of me; for I am meek and lowly in heart: and ye shall find rest unto your souls"* (Matthew 11:29). A disciple is an ardent follower of a leader in all things. Discipleship is the process of following a master, learning from a teacher or imitating a leader. True Christian discipleship, therefore, can be defined as following in the steps of Christ. It means learning from Jesus, living like Christ, walking and working like our Lord Jesus. (Read John 13:13-15; 1 John 2:6)

The Importance of Christian Discipleship: *"… the disciples were called Christians first in Antioch… Ye are witnesses, and God also, how holily and justly and unblameably we behaved ourselves among you that believe:"* (Acts 11:26; 1 Thessalonians 2:10).

True Christian discipleship is essential because it is transformational in nature reflecting the life of Christ as the case was in Antioch when the disciples were first called 'Christians' due to their lifestyle of Christlikeness, Godliness, holiness, purity, righteousness, sanctity and blamelessness. This lends credence to the fact that true

Christian discipleship eliminates spiritual prodigality and moral irresponsibility thus providing responsive leadership and followership through forensic righteousness as obtainable in the early church as a blueprint for the church today. *"For I say unto you, That except your righteousness shall exceed the righteousness of the scribes and Pharisees, ye shall in no case enter into the kingdom of heaven."* (Matthew 5:20)

Prerequisites to Christian Discipleship: There are experiences that should precede and qualify anyone for the journey of true discipleship. It demands and begins with the prerequisite of genuine salvation supported with justification, sanctification and baptism of the Holy Ghost. *"Depart ye, depart ye, go ye out from thence, touch no unclean thing; go ye out of the midst of her; be ye clean, that bear the vessels of the LORD"* (Isaiah 52:11).

Then, the disciple must count the cost of carrying the cross joyfully with understanding that sanctity comes before service and character precedes charisma at all times (Read Matthew 6:33; 10:37-39;) *"Then said Jesus unto his disciples, If any man will come after me, let him deny himself, and take up his cross, and follow me...So likewise, whosoever he be of you that forsaketh not all that he hath, he cannot be my disciple. Salt is good: but if the salt have lost his savour, wherewith shall it be seasoned? It is neither fit for the land, nor yet for the dunghill; but men cast it out. He that hath ears to hear, let him hear"* (Matthew 16:24; Luke 14:33-35).

In the terms of service, the true Christian disciple totally forsakes all in order to focus on his stewardship as a caretaker and manager who sacrifices his time, money, wealth, knowledge, property and even his life and does not go on holidays, recess or retirement because discipleship is a continuous lifelong thing. *"Let a man so account of us, as of the ministers of Christ, and stewards of the mysteries of God. Moreover it is required in stewards, that a man be found faithful….Then said Jesus to those Jews which believed on him, If ye continue in my word, then are ye my disciples indeed;…And ye shall be hated of all men for my name's sake: but he that endureth to the end shall be saved"* (1 Corinthians 4:1-2; John 8:31; Matthew 10:22). It could be said that a true disciple of Christ is a living martyr! *"For whosoever will save his life shall lose it; but whosoever shall lose his life for my sake and the gospel's, the same shall save it."* (Mark 8:35)

Hindrances to Christian Discipleship: *"And take heed to yourselves, lest at any time your hearts be overcharged with surfeiting, and drunkenness, and cares of this life, and so that day come upon you unawares"* (Luke 21:34).

Worldliness, misplaced priorities, earthly comforts and pleasures; and the deception of operational gifts constitute a great hindrance and disqualify the disciple. These are summed up as the lust of the flesh, the lust of the eyes and the pride of life. *"He that loveth father or mother more than me is not worthy of me: and he that loveth son* or daughter more than me is not worthy of me… *Love not the world, neither the things that are in the world. If any man love the world, the love of the Father is not in him… Ye adulterers and adulteresses, know ye not that the friendship of the world is enmity with God? whosoever therefore will be a friend of the world is the enemy of God… Not every one that saith unto me, Lord, Lord, shall enter into the kingdom of heaven; but he that doeth the will of my Father which is in heaven. Many will say to me in that day, Lord, Lord, have we not prophesied in thy name? and in thy name have cast out devils? and in thy name done many wonderful works? And then will I profess unto them, I never knew you: depart from me, ye that work iniquity…"* (Matthew 10:37; 1 John 2:15-17; James 4:4; Matthew 7:21-23)

Rewards of Christian Discipleship: *"And Jesus answered and said, Verily I say unto you, There is no man that hath left house, or brethren, or sisters, or father, or mother, or wife, or children, or lands, for my sake, and the gospel's, But he shall receive an hundredfold now in this time, houses, and brethren, and sisters, and mothers, and children, and lands, with persecutions; and in the world to come eternal life"* (Mark 10:29-30).

An unimaginable degree of multiplicity of unfathomable real abundance from the Almighty unfailing God awaits the faithful disciple. *"But as it is written, Eye hath not seen, nor ear heard, neither have entered into the heart of man, the things which God hath prepared for them that love him."* (1

Corinthians 2:9). There are about five crowns the crown of life, the crown of righteousness, the crown of glory, the incorruptible crown and the crown of rejoicing; and much more for the victorious disciple.

*"Blessed is the man that endureth temptation: for when he is tried, he shall receive **the crown of life**, which the Lord hath promised to them that love him… Fear none of those things which thou shalt suffer: behold, the devil shall cast some of you into prison, that ye may be tried; and ye shall have tribulation ten days: be thou faithful unto death, and I will give thee **a crown of life**."* (James 1:12; Revelation 2:10)

*"Henceforth there is laid up for me **a crown of righteousness**, which the Lord, the righteous judge, shall give me at that day: and not to me only, but unto all them also that love his appearing."* (2 Timothy 4:8)

*"And when the chief Shepherd shall appear, ye shall receive **a crown of glory** that fadeth not away."* (1 Peter 5:4; Also Isaiah 28:5; 62:3)

*"And every man that striveth for the mastery is temperate in all things. Now they do it to obtain a corruptible crown; but we **an incorruptible**."* (1 Corinthians 9:25; 1 Peter 11:4)

*"For what is our hope, or joy, or **crown of rejoicing**? Are not even ye in the presence of our Lord Jesus Christ at his coming?"* (1 Thessalonians 2:19; Revelation 12:1)

CHAPTER SEVEN

THE HOLY SPIRIT POWER

"And it shall come to pass afterward, that I will pour out my spirit upon all flesh; and your sons and your daughters shall prophesy, your old men shall dream dreams, your young men shall see visions... And I will pray the Father, and he shall give you another Comforter, that he may abide with you forever... But the Comforter, which is the Holy Ghost, whom the Father will send in my name, he shall teach you all things, and bring all things to your remembrance, whatsoever I have said unto you... But ye shall receive power, after that the Holy Ghost is come upon you: and ye shall be witnesses unto me both in Jerusalem, and in all Judaea, and in Samaria, and unto the uttermost part of the earth" (Joel 2:28; John 14:16, 26; Acts 1:8).

The Holy Spirit is the Spirit of the living God. He took part in the creation of the world and man. He is the Spirit power that comes upon every child of God. God promised in the Old Testament in the book of Joel 2:28 that He would send the Holy Spirit to the believers. He fulfilled the promise in the New Testament in Acts 2:4, 16, *"And they were all filled with the Holy Ghost, and began to speak with other tongues, as the Spirit gave them utterance...But this is that which was spoken by the prophet Joel."* The Promise is for every sanctified child of God today.

"Now the God of hope fill you with all joy and peace in believing, that ye may abound in hope, through the power of the Holy Ghost." (Romans 15:13)

Pre-requisites to the Holy Spirit Baptism

Baptism of the Holy Spirit is not for everybody. The Spirit is for a peculiar people, that is, those who are born again while the sinners are left out completely. Therefore, the Spirit's guarantee for Holy Ghost Baptism includes the following:

a. Evidence of Salvation

"And Zacchaeus stood, and said unto the Lord; Behold, Lord, the half of my goods I give to the poor; and if I have taken anything from any man by false accusation, I restore

him fourfold… Now when they heard this, they were pricked in their heart, and said unto Peter and to the rest of the apostles, Men and brethren, what shall we do? Then Peter said unto them, Repent, and be baptized every one of you in the name of Jesus Christ for the remission of sins, and ye shall receive the gift of the Holy Ghost" (Luke 19:8; Acts 2:37-38). When salvation comes, it will transform and change you, for old things are passed away and all things are become new. If you are saved, you will be willing to do your restitution and hate the sinful things that you used to love before.

b. Evidence of Holiness and Sanctification

The Holy Spirit cannot dwell in an unclean vessel; therefore, you must be purified. *"Sanctify them through thy truth: thy word is truth…And the very God of peace sanctify you wholly; and I pray God your whole spirit and soul and body be preserved blameless unto the coming of our Lord Jesus Christ"* (John 17:17; 1Thesalonians 5:23). If sanctification is not important, Our Lord Jesus Christ and Apostle Paul wouldn't have prayed for it.

c. Unity with the Church as the Body of Christ

"That they all may be one; as thou, Father, art in me, and I in thee, that they also may be one in us: that the world may believe that thou hast sent me" (John 17:21). No wonder, Jesus prayed for the unity of the brethren (Church). It is a great evidence of sanctification. The clear evidence

of unity was seen in the early church before they received the Spirit's baptism gift. *"And when the day of Pentecost was fully come, they were all with one accord in one place. And suddenly there came a sound from heaven as of a rushing mighty wind, and it filled all the house where they were sitting"* (Acts 2:1-2).

Purpose of the Holy Spirit Baptism

"And I will pray the Father, and he shall give you another Comforter, that he may abide with you for ever...But when the Comforter is come, whom I will send unto you from the Father, even the Spirit of truth, which proceedeth from the Father, he shall testify of me" (John 14:16; 15:26).

It helps to accomplish the goals, commands and also, the promises of God. *"But ye shall receive power, after that the Holy Ghost is come upon you: and ye shall be witnesses unto me both in Jerusalem, and in all Judaea, and in Samaria, and unto the uttermost part of the earth"* (Acts 1:8). It helps us in prayer. *"Likewise the Spirit also helpeth our infirmities: for we know not what we should pray for as we ought: but the Spirit itself maketh intercession for us with groanings which cannot be uttered. And he that searcheth the hearts knoweth what is the mind of the Spirit, because he maketh intercession for the saints according to the will of God. And we know that all things work together for good to them that love God, to them who are the called according to his purpose"* (Romans 8:26-28).

Many Christians have the zeal and appetite to pray but there's no driving force to accomplish their zeal. Yet, being baptized in the Holy Ghost will help us to live a victorious Christian life. Likewise, it quickens the soul and body for revival. *"It is the spirit that quickeneth; the flesh profiteth nothing: the words that I speak unto you, they are spirit, and they are life"* (John 6:63).

The Spirit brings the word of God to our remembrance and gives us revelation. Through the Spirit of God, we take the right decision in life and obtain direction by the vision of God. *"For as many as are led by the Spirit of God, they are the sons of God. For ye have not received the spirit of bondage again to fear; but ye have received the Spirit of adoption, whereby we cry, Abba, Father. The Spirit itself beareth witness with our spirit, that we are the children of God"* (Romans 8:14-16).

Promised Power from God

"And, behold, I send the promise of my Father upon you: but tarry ye in the city of Jerusalem, until ye be endued with power from on high...But ye shall receive power, after that the Holy Ghost is come upon you: and ye shall be witnesses unto me both in Jerusalem, and in all Judaea, and in Samaria, and unto the uttermost part of the earth" (Luke 24:49; Acts 1:8).

God has promised to give us power these Last Days (Joel

2:28). It is the power to do the work of God. The power is often evidenced with the sign of a new tongue, not only for the Apostles but for everyone that believes in the name of Jesus. *"While Peter yet spake these words, the Holy Ghost fell on all them which heard the word"* (Acts 10:44).

CHAPTER EIGHT

DEFINING THE GIFTS OF THE SPIRIT

"*Now there are diversities of gifts, but the same Spirit. And there are differences of administrations, but the same Lord. And there are diversities of operations, but it is the same God which worketh all in all. But the manifestation of the Spirit is given to every man to profit withal. For to one is given by the Spirit the word of wisdom; to another the word of knowledge by the same Spirit; To another faith by the same Spirit; to another the gifts of healing by the same Spirit; To another the working of miracles; to another prophecy; to another discerning of spirits; to another divers kinds of tongues; to another the interpretation of tongues: But all these worketh that one and the selfsame Spirit, dividing to every man severally as he will ... Wherefore he saith, when he ascended up on high, he led captivity captive, and gave gifts unto men. (Now that he ascended, what is it but that he also descended first into the lower parts of the earth? He that descended is the same also that ascended up far above all heavens, that he might fill all things.) And he gave some, apostles; and some, prophets; and some, evangelists; and some, pastors and teachers"* (1 Corinthians 12:4-11; Ephesians 4:8-11).

Baptism with Holy Spirit is different from the Gifts of the Holy Spirit that are given to empower and edify the Church; and to glorify God. The Holy Spirit is a Person while His gifts are bequeathed to believers for edification and evangelization. To get the gifts of God, you must thirst for it until the latter rain begins to fall on you. These gifts can be classified into three:

GIFTS OF REVELATION

The spiritual gifts that can be classified under this group are
:

The Word of Wisdom - The word of wisdom is a supernatural manifestation of God's wisdom at the time it is needed for a particular purpose. Such a believer has the ability to apply the principles of the Word of God in a practical way to specific situations and to recommend the best course of action at the best time. Christian Counsellors operate this gift regularly. A Biblical typology is the case where King Solomon was able to identify the rightful mother of the living child in contest between two harlots. (1 Kings 3:16-28)

The Word of Knowledge - The word of knowledge is the divine revelation of the supernatural act of God. Knowledge is the raw facts revealed, while wisdom is the right use of the knowledge for edification and benefits of the church at large. This is the divine ability to discover secret things, analyze it and systematize the truth for the benefit of others. Jesus demonstrated this when He perceived and knew that virtue had gone out of Him to heal the woman with the issue of blood who had touched Him secretly in a crowd. (Luke 8:42-48)

The Discerning of Spirits - The gift of discernment is a supernatural insight into the realm of the spirits to detect and to clearly discern the spirit of truth and the spirit of error in the church. This is neither suspicion nor imagination. These gifts are needed to guide decision-making in church matters. An instance was when the Holy Ghost picked out Barnabas and Saul for a missionary adventure. Another one was when Paul discerned and delivered the damsel possessed with the spirit of divination. The devil may speak facts but he will never tell the truth and we must know the difference (Acts 13:1-4; 16:16-18; John 8:44)

GIFTS OF POWER

The gifts under this group are:

The Gift of Faith - The supernatural manifestation of the assurance of answer to prayer in unusual situations, the gift of faith is the extraordinary faith to do exploit for the benefits of the Church. *"And Jesus said unto them, Because of your unbelief: for verily I say unto you, If ye have faith as a grain of mustard seed, ye shall say unto this mountain, Remove hence to yonder place; and it shall remove; and nothing shall be impossible unto you... And the Lord said, If ye had faith as a grain of mustard seed, ye might say unto this sycamine tree, Be thou plucked up by the root, and be thou planted in the sea; and it should obey you."* (Matthew 17:20; Luke 17:6)

The Gift of Healing It's the supernatural manifestation of the power of God to heal the sick or an ability to serve as a human instrument through whom God supernaturally cures illnesses and restores health. *"Insomuch that they brought forth the sick into the streets, and laid them on beds and couches, that at the least the shadow of Peter passing by might overshadow some of them. There came also a multitude out of the cities round about unto Jerusalem, bringing sick folks, and them which were vexed with unclean* *spirits: and they were healed every one."* (Acts 5:15-16)

The Working of Miracles - The working of miracles is a supernatural manifestation of powerful works. This gift is not outdated and did not die with the Apostles as it still operates until today. Miracles bear witness to God's abiding presence and the truth of His proclaimed Word by His faithful servant. The powerful works wrought through this gift include raising the dead and miraculous alteration of circumstances. *"And God wrought special miracles by the hands of Paul: So that from his body were brought unto the sick handkerchiefs or aprons, and the diseases departed from them, and the evil spirits went out of them"* (Acts 19:11-12)

GIFTS OF INSPIRATION

This consists of:

The Gift of Prophecy Prophecy is a gift of the Spirit that can come to any member of the body of Christ. It's a supernatural utterance not learned or trained to speak but by the Spirit of God. It is the ability to receive the word from God and proclaim the message to the member(s) or body of Christ. *"Having then gifts differing according to the grace that is given to us, whether prophecy, let us prophesy according to the proportion of faith;"* (Romans 12:6)

Diverse Kinds of Tongues   It's a supernatural manifestation by way of utterances in languages not known to the speaker in different ways. *"What is it then? I will pray with the spirit, and I will pray with the understanding also: I will sing with the spirit, and I will sing with the understanding also. Else when thou shalt bless with the spirit, how shall he that occupieth the room of the unlearned say Amen at thy giving of thanks, seeing he understandeth not what thou sayest? For thou verily givest thanks well, but the other is not edified. Yet in the church I had rather speak five words with my understanding, that by my voice I might teach others also, than ten thousand words in an unknown tongue."* (1 Corinthian 14:15-19)

Interpretation of Tongues - The gift of interpretation of tongues is a supernatural utterance of interpretation of unknown languages to the one speaking or to the hearers. In other words, it is ability to translate into the vernacular, a message publicly uttered in a tongue. *"I would that ye all spake with tongues, but rather that ye prophesied: for greater is he that prophesieth than he that speaketh with tongues, except he interpret, that the church may receive edifying. Wherefore let him that speaketh in an unknown tongue pray that he may interpret. If any man speak in an unknown tongue, let it be by two, or at the most by three, and that by course; and let one interpret."* (1 Corinthians 14:5, 13, 27)

These gifts can also be called Vocal gifts.

"And God hath set some in the church, first apostles, secondarily prophets, thirdly teachers, after that miracles, then gifts of healings, helps, governments, diversities of tongues. Are all apostles? are all prophets? are all teachers? are all workers of miracles? Have all the gifts of healing? do all speak with tongues? do all interpret? But covet earnestly the best gifts: and yet shew I unto you a more excellent way." (1 Corinthians 12:28-30)

CHAPTER NINE

DANIEL - AN UNCOMPROMISING BELIEVER

"Blessed are the undefiled in the way, who walk in the law of the Lord... But Daniel purposed in his heart that he would not defile himself with the portion of the king's meat, nor with the wine which he drank: therefore he requested of the prince of the eunuchs that he might not defile himself. Now God had brought Daniel into favour and tender love with the prince of the eunuchs. And the prince of the eunuchs said unto Daniel, I fear my lord the king, who hath appointed your meat and your drink: for why should he see your faces worse liking than the children which are of your sort? then shall ye make me endanger my head to the king. Then said Daniel to Melzar, whom the prince of the eunuchs had set over

Daniel, Hananiah, Mishael, and Azariah, Prove thy servants, I beseech thee, ten days; and let them give us pulse to eat, and water to drink. Then let our countenances be looked upon before thee, and the countenance of the children that eat of the portion of the king's meat: and as thou seest, deal with thy servants. So he consented to them in this matter, and proved them ten days. And at the end of ten days their countenances appeared fairer and fatter in flesh than all the children which did eat the portion of the king's meat. Thus, Melzar took away the portion of their meat, and the wine that they should drink; and gave them pulse. As for these four children, God gave them knowledge and skill in all learning and wisdom: and Daniel had understanding in all visions and dreams. Now at the end of the days that the king had said he should bring them in, then the prince of the eunuchs brought them in before Nebuchadnezzar. And the king communed with them; and among them all was found none like Daniel, Hananiah, Mishael, and Azariah: therefore stood they before the king. And in all matters of wisdom and understanding, that the king enquired of them, he found them ten times better than all the magicians and astrologers that were in all his realm. And Daniel continued even unto the first year of king Cyrus" (Psalms 119:1; Daniel 1:8-21).

Daniel was among the Jews carried captive to Babylon by King Nebuchadnezzar during the reign of Jehoiakim, King of Judah. He was probably a noble descent (Daniel 1:3) and a teenager when Nebuchadnezzar sacked Jerusalem and wiped out the sovereignty of Judah. In Babylon, Daniel was drafted to serve as a minister in a Babylonian cabinet. While in training, he was found ten times better in wisdom and understanding than all the native magicians and astrologers and was especially gifted in "understanding of all visions and dreams" (Daniel 1:17).

Daniel's interpretation of dreams earned him the post of Prime Minister under Nebuchadnezzar and his son, Belshazzar. Daniel continued to serve in the government of the nation and rose to the post of first President under King Darius in the Medo-Persian Empire. (Daniel 6:1-3). In any position and under any regime, Daniel kept his faith, preserved his purity and maintained his convictions in the Lord.

Unashamed Boldness

"I will speak of thy testimonies also before kings, and will not be ashamed... So that we may boldly say, The Lord is my helper, and I will not fear what man shall do unto me" (Psalms 11:46; Hebrews 13:6).

Unashamed boldness goes along with uncompromising lifestyle. With purpose of heart like Daniel, he resisted the strong and overwhelming temptation of his days which was also peculiar to every believer of today. *"The fear of* man bringeth a snare...Whosoever therefore shall be ashamed of me and of my words in this adulterous and sinful generation; of him also shall the Son of man be ashamed, when he cometh in the glory of his Father with the holy angels" (Proverbs 29:25; Mark 8:38). Daniel, in his own time, thoroughly and irrevocably made up his mind. Therefore, we must watch against any compromise that can mire our Christianity.

"Be ye not unequally yoked together with unbelievers: for what fellowship hath righteousness with unrighteousness? and what communion hath light with darkness? And what concord hath Christ with Belial? or what part hath he that believeth with an infidel? And what agreement hath the temple of God with idols? for ye are the temple of the living God; as God hath said, I will dwell in them, and walk in them; and I will be their God, and they shall be my people. Wherefore come out from among them, and be ye separate, saith the Lord, and touch not the unclean thing; and I will receive you. And will be a Father unto you, and ye shall be my sons and daughters, saith the Lord Almighty" (2 Corinthians 6:14-18).

We can join Daniel to decide in our hearts not to compromise. There are examples for us to follow in the Bible;

Joseph   "And it came to pass after these things, that his master's wife cast her eyes upon Joseph; and she said, Lie with me. *But he refused, and said unto his master's wife, Behold, my master wotteth not what is with me in the house, and he hath committed all that he hath to my hand; There is none greater in this house than I; neither hath he kept back any thing from me but thee, because thou art his wife: how then can I do this great wickedness, and sin against God?"* (Genesis 39:7-9);

Job *"Then said his wife unto him, Dost thou still retain thine integrity? curse God, and die. But he said unto her, Thou speakest as one of the foolish women speaketh. What? shall we receive good at the hand of God, and shall we not receive evil? In all this did not Job sin with his lips"* (Job 2:9-10).

Shadrach, Meshach and Abednego *"Then Nebuchadnezzar in his rage and fury commanded to bring Shadrach, Meshach, and Abednego. Then they brought these men before the king. Nebuchadnezzar spake and said unto them, Is it true, O Shadrach, Meshach, and Abednego, do not ye serve my gods, nor worship the golden image which I have set up? Now if ye be ready that at what time ye hear the sound of the cornet, flute, harp, sackbut, psaltery, and dulcimer, and all kinds of musick, ye fall down and worship the image which I have made; well: but if ye worship not, ye shall be cast the same hour into the midst of a burning fiery furnace; and who is that God that shall deliver you out of my hands? Shadrach, Meshach, and Abednego, answered and said to the king, O Nebuchadnezzar, we are not careful to answer thee in this matter. If it be so, our God whom we serve is able to deliver us from the burning fiery furnace, and he will deliver us out of thine hand, O king. But if not, be it known unto thee, O king, that we will not serve thy gods, nor worship the golden image which thou hast set up.*" (Daniel 3:13-18); and Paul (Acts 21:10-14). To be strengthened against compromise like Daniel, the following are absolutely necessary:

a. Daily reading of God's word and full persuasion on Biblical convictions. "*Wherewithal shall a young man cleanse his way? by taking heed thereto according to thy word… Thy word have I hid in mine heart, that I might not sin against thee… Therefore I esteem all thy precepts concerning all things to be right; and I hate every false way*" (Psalms 119:9, 11, 128).

b. A fixed heart on Biblical convictions. "*My heart is fixed, O God, my heart is fixed: I will sing and give praise… For I am persuaded, that neither death, nor life, nor angels, nor principalities, nor powers, nor things present, nor things to come, Nor height, nor depth, nor any other creature, shall be able to separate us from the love of God, which is in Christ Jesus our Lord*" (Psalms 57:7; Romans 8:38-39).

c. Watchfulness over choice of companions. "*Be not deceived: evil communications corrupt good manners… My son, if sinners entice thee, consent thou not*" (Proverbs 1:10; 1 Corinthians 15:33).

d. Self-crucifixion. "*I am crucified with Christ: nevertheless I* live; yet not I, but Christ liveth in me: and the life which I now live in the flesh I live by the faith of the Son of God, who loved me, and gave himself for me"* (Galatians 2:20).

e. Daily dependence on God's grace. *"Looking unto Jesus the author and finisher of our faith; who for the joy that was set before him endured the cross, despising the shame, and is set down at the right hand of the throne of God"* (Hebrews 12:2).

Uncommon Standard

"Abstain from all appearance of evil... All things are lawful for me, but all things are not expedient: all things are lawful for me, but all things edify not" (1 Thessalonians 5:22; 1 Corinthians 10:23).

Believers who aim to please God do not live self-indulgence lives. They do not do things the way everybody does. They live up to the standard of the word of God which is always above that of the average professing, nominal Christian.

Daniel clearly distinguished himself from all gluttons and drunkards in Babylon. He, as a Bible believer, knew the evil effects of strong drinks.

"Now therefore beware, I pray thee, and drink not wine nor strong drink, and eat not any unclean thing… Woe unto them that rise up early in the morning, that they may follow strong drink; that continue until night, till wine inflame them!... Woe

unto them that are mighty to drink wine, and men of strength to mingle strong drink" (Judges 13:4; Isaiah 5:11, 22).

Daniel and his companions though young, knew that self-restraint is the surest path to health, usefulness and joy. Besides, the foods and wines had been dedicated to the Babylonian idols. How could they eat such foods, drink such wines and still preserve their holiness unto the true God?

Unparallel Protection

"Now God had brought Daniel into favour and tender love with the prince of the eunuchs... He made them also to be pitied of all those that carried them captives... And who is he that will harm you, if ye be followers of that which is good?" (Daniel 1:9; Psalms 106:46; 1 Peter 3:13).

God protects those who are committed to Him. When you compromise, you lose God's protection and you are on your own. When anybody stands up and lives up to a biblical standard like Daniel, God is always on his side. And when God says you live, none can take your life or what has graciously given you. God of all possibility can sway Kings, nobles and the whole society to your support.

Unhindered Persistence

"And the Lord spake unto Moses, saying, Go in, speak

unto Pharaoh king of Egypt, that he let the children of Israel go out of his land... And the prince of the eunuchs said unto Daniel, I fear my lord the king, who hath appointed your meat and your drink: for why should he see your faces worse liking than the children which are of your sort? then shall ye make me endanger my head to the king. Then said Daniel to Melzar, whom the prince of the eunuchs had set over Daniel, Hananiah, Mishael, and Azariah Prove thy servants, I beseech thee, ten days; and let them give us pulse to eat, and water to drink" (Exodus 5:1-2; Daniel 1:10-12).

An uncompromising person never gives up. When the first doors close, he doesn't give up. Having made up his mind, he blended gentleness with firm principles. With the temporary refusal of Ashpenaz, Daniel, approached Melzar.

Unblemished Faith

"All the paths of the Lord are mercy and truth unto such as keep his covenant and his testimonies. Let us hold fast the profession of our faith without wavering; for he is faithful that promised" (Psalms 25:10; Hebrews 10:23).

Sin brings doubt but the purity of life brings confidence in God. When the heart is pure, faith is strong. No matter who gets angry for your uncompromising stand, if you take your stand with God's word, He will stand by you. One with God is more than the majority.

Unusual Test

"So he consented to them in this matter, and proved them ten days. And at the end of ten days their countenances appeared fairer and fatter in flesh than all the children which did eat the portion of the king's meat. ThusMelzar took away the portion of their meat, and the wine that they should drink; and gave them pulse... For as many as are led by the Spirit of God, they are the sons of God" (Daniel 1:14-16; Romans 8:14).

Daniel proposed only an experiment for ten days. This issue was brought to the test of practical demonstration. Daniel proposed this test in the exercise of full confidence in God and it worked for him.

Immeasurable Blessing

"And said, If thou wilt diligently hearken to the voice of the Lord thy God, and wilt do that which is right in his sight, and wilt give ear to his commandments, and keep all his statutes, I will put none of these diseases upon thee, which I have brought upon the Egyptians: for I am the Lord that healeth thee... Jesus answered and said unto him, If a man love me, he will keep my words: and my Father will love him, and we will come unto him, and make our abode with him... For ye have need of patience, that, after ye have done the will of God, ye might receive the promise" (Exodus 15:26; John 14:23; Hebrews 10:36).

God's sovereign blessings depend on man's total commitment. Physical health and vigor, intellectual attainment and strength, moral and spiritual power, together with continual prosperity and influence came on Daniel and his peers for their uncompromising stand and faith in God.

CHAPTER TEN

THE ESSENCE OF PRAYER

"And in the morning, rising up a great while before day, he went out, and departed into a solitary place, and there prayed... And it came to pass in those days, that he went out into a mountain to pray, and continued all night in prayer to God. And when it was day, he called unto him his disciples: and of them he chose twelve, whom also he named apostles" (Mark 1:35; Luke 6:12, 13).

Our Lord Jesus Christ taught us the necessity of praying as his ministry was characterized with result-oriented prayer leading to the manifestation of signs and wonders. Thomas Buxton warned, "You know the value of prayer; it's precious beyond all price. Never, never neglect it." In Acts 6:1-4,

"And in those days when the number of the disciples was multiplied, there arose a murmuring of the Grecians against the Hebrews because their widows were neglected in the daily ministration. Then the twelve called the multitude of the disciples unto them, and said, It is not a reason that we should leave the word of God, and serve tables. Wherefore, brethren, look ye out among you seven men of honest report, full of the Holy Ghost and wisdom, whom we may appoint over this business. But we will give ourselves continually to prayer, and to the ministry of the word." Through Prayers:

Faith is generated and manifested in the lives of the members of the church to believe God for the impossible.

War is waged against the temptations and attacks of the devil and his demons.

Great mysteries are revealed to God's children; *"for surely the Lord God will do nothing, but He revealeth His secret unto His servants the prophets"* (Amos 3:7; Daniel 2:14-19).

Men are shaped for God through prayer. Men of zeal, courage and unwavering boldness are developed through prayers (Acts 4:13, 23-31).

In 1540, Luther's friend, (Friedrich Myconius) at the point of death, sent a farewell note to him. When Luther got the letter, he prayed and instantly sent back a reply: "I command thee in the name of God to live; I still have need of thee in the work of reforming the churches. The Lord will never let me hear that thou art dead but will permit thee to survive me. For this, I am praying and it will be done because I seek only to glorify the name of God." History tells us that this prayer was answered accordingly. Every believer should bear the burdens of others by involving in the prayer ministry (Ephesians 1:15, 16; Colossians 1:3, 9-19) which aims at bringing the perfect will of God to the lives of the people. Such prayers should focus on:

1. Fellow believers (Colossians 1:9-12; James 5:16; Romans 1:9).

2. Ministers of the Word (Colossians 4:3; 2 Thessalonians 3:12).

3. New converts (1Thessalonians 3:9-13).

4. Sick brethren (James 5:14-16).

5. Backsliders (1 John 5:16; Exodus 32:31-32).

6. Rulers and kings (1Timothy 2:1-2).

7. Cities where we live (Jeremiah 29:7; Psalm 122:6).

8. Our persecutors and enemies (Luke 6:27-28; Matthew 5:44).

9. Our nation (Romans 10:1; Isaiah 62:67).

10. All saints (Ephesians 6:8).

11. Ourselves (Matthew 6:6).

Other matters the faithful prayer minister should include in his prayers are:

a. Revival of God's work and his people (Habakkuk 3:2)

b. More labourers and effectiveness in God's vineyard (Matthew 9:38; Ephesians 6:19).

c. Open doors for greater outreach (1 Corinthians 16:19; 2 Corinthians 2:12).

d. Conviction of sin for the unsaved (Acts 8:22; Psalm 1:16).

e. Sanctification of believers (1 Thessalonians 5:23).

f. Gift of the Holy Spirit (Luke 11:13; Acts 8:15).

g. Healing and deliverance for the oppressed (James 5:14-16).

h. Wisdom and understanding for the saints (Ephesians 1:16-19).

i. Preservation from evil (Psalm 18:8-9; John 17:15).

J. Provision for every need (Philippians 4:6, 19).

Praying Men in the Bible

Colossians 4:12, "*Epaphras, who is one of you, a servant of Christ, saluteth you, always labouring fervently for you in prayers, that ye may stand perfect and complete in all the will of God.*"

Examples abound in the Scriptures of men who made an indelible print, changed circumstances, stopped the mouth of lions, received revelations and did exploits for their Lord. God is looking for such men and women in this end time men who will still the congregation of doubters, men who will persevere until there is a sign of the abundance of rain.

Men of fervency and unwavering faith who will never let Him go until there's a blessing, men who will constantly fight spiritual battles against sin, against the desire of the flesh, against false doctrines, unscriptural practices and against all oppositions of satan to the ministry committed to our hands. *"And say to Archippus, Take heed to the ministry which thou hast received in the Lord, that thou fulfil it."* (Colossians 4:17).

Experiencing and Maintaining a Prayer Life

"And he spake a parable unto them to this end, that men ought always to pray, and not to faint... Then came the disciples to Jesus apart, and said, Why could not we cast him out? And Jesus said unto them, Because of your unbelief: for verily I say unto you, If ye have faith as a grain of mustard seed, ye shall say unto this mountain, Remove hence to yonder place; and it shall remove; and nothing shall be impossible unto you. Howbeit this kind goeth not out but by prayer and fasting... Watch and pray, that ye enter not into temptation: the spirit indeed

is willing, but the flesh is weak... Continue in prayer, and watch in the same with thanksgiving" (Luke 18:1; Matthew 17:19-21; 26:41; Colossians 4:2).

The challenging prayer life of our Lord Jesus Christ should be the model for every believer to follow. As the disciples of old did, we should humbly ask the Lord to teach us to pray. It's not enough to pray now, we must continue persistently in prayer until it becomes a habit, a duty and an expression of our relationship with God. If we are to maintain a prayer ministry, there must be great determination, discipline, self-denial and faith. *"But let him ask in faith, nothing wavering. For he that wavereth is like a wave of the sea driven with the wind and tossed"* (James 1:6). Watchfulness is also necessary (Mark 14:38).

We must always avoid sin because sin in any form will hinder us from attaining the height of our prayer ministry. *"If I regard iniquity in my heart, the Lord will not hear me"* (Psalm 66:18). The spirit of jealousy or unforgiveness, grudge and bitterness desire for retaliation will break the wings of faith and hush the cry of real prayer. *"Therefore I say unto you, What things soever ye desire, when ye pray, believe that ye receive them, and ye shall have them. And when ye stand praying, forgive, if ye have ought against any: that your Father also which is in heaven may forgive you your trespasses. But if ye do not forgive, neither will your Father which is in heaven forgive your trespasses"* (Mark 11:24-26). A callous conscience concerning some unpaid debt, defrauding Government in tax payment or dodging an act of restitution could hinder the incoming grace tide of blessings from many a soul. *"He that turneth away his ear from hearing the law, even his prayer shall be abomination"* (Proverbs 28:9). If God will do nothing but by answer to prayer, then, prayer is the potent weapon and key to realizing our dreams and doing the impossible. Let us pray always.

CHAPTER ELEVEN

PRAYER POWER

The Infinite, Almighty God is able to give great answers to prayers. God cannot sin or lie or be tempted. God can do anything by His infinite power and authority. He delights in granting prayers for big things if He could give His only son. *"He that spared not his own Son, but delivered him up for us all, how shall he not with him also freely give us all things?"* (Romans 8:32). Never was any man found to ask too much of God. We have not because we ask not.

Command to Ask Great Things

"I am the Lord thy God, which brought thee out of the land of Egypt: open thy mouth wide, and I will fill it...

Call unto me, and I will answer thee, and show thee great and mighty things, which thou knowest not" (Psalms 81:10; Jeremiah 33:3).

We have little because we ask little. If we would open our mouths wider, we would get bigger things from God. Nothing is impossible with Him. *"And Jesus said unto them, Because of your unbelief: for verily I say unto you, If ye have faith as a grain of mustard seed, ye shall say unto this mountain, Remove hence to yonder place; and it shall remove; and nothing shall be impossible unto you"* Matthew 17:20).

Bible examples of great things

Joshua commanded the sun to stand still. *"Then spake Joshua to the Lord in the day when the Lord delivered up the Amorites before the children of Israel, and he said in the sight of Israel, Sun, stand thou still upon Gibeon; and thou, Moon, in the valley of Ajalon. And the sun stood still, and the moon stayed, until the people had avenged themselves upon their enemies. Is not this written in the book of Jasher? So the sun stood still in the midst of heaven, and hasted not to go down about a whole day. And there was no day like that before it or after it, that the Lord hearkened unto the voice of a man: for the Lord fought for Israel"* (Joshua 10:12-14).

Elisha's double portion from Elijah. In the Book of 2 Kings 2:1-14, Elisha would not be discouraged but sought for a double portion of Elijah's anointing. Elijah had only one portion yet Elisha made two out of that.

The increase of the pot of oil. The amount of oil that the widow of one of the sons of the prophets got was the number of vessels she had. God has more oil than she had vessels and the oil did not stop until there was nowhere to put it (2 Kings 4:1-7).

Blessings of Big Prayers

Prayer is big enough when it glorifies God and shows His great power. "*And when all the people saw it, they fell on their faces: and they said, The Lord, he is the God; the Lord, he is the God... And he could there do no mighty work, save that he laid his hands upon a few sick folk, and healed them*" (1 Kings 18:39; Mark 6:5).

Big praying prospers God's work: "*Ask of me, and I shall give thee the heathen for thine inheritance, and the uttermost parts of the earth for thy possession*" (Psalms 2:8). The work of God languishes because of our small asking. Congregations dwindle because they refuse to practice asking big things from God.

You will get what you need according to Jeremiah 33:3 when you pray for great things. God's people live in poverty, sickness, disappointment and defeat because they do not pray for a big things.

Importunate Prevailing Prayer

"And he said unto them, Which of you shall have a friend, and shall go unto him at midnight, and say unto him, Friend, lend me three loaves; For a friend of mine in his journey is come to me, and I have nothing to set before him? And he from within shall answer and say, Trouble me not: the door is now shut, and my children are with me in bed; I cannot rise and give thee. I say unto you, Though he will not rise and give him, because he is his friend, yet because of his importunity he will rise and give him as many as he needeth. And I say unto you, Ask, and it shall be given you; seek, and ye shall find; knock, and it shall be opened unto you. For every one that asketh receiveth; and he that seeketh findeth; and to him that knocketh it shall be opened. If a son shall ask bread of any of you that is a father, will he give him a stone? or if he ask a fish, will he for a fish give him a serpent? Or if he shall ask an egg, will he offer him a scorpion? If ye then, being evil, know how to give good gifts unto your children: how much more shall your heavenly Father give the Holy Spirit to them that ask him?" (Luke 11:5-13).

The Bible is filled with the stories of men and women who prayed through in one particular situation or the other. They refused to take 'NO' for the answer to their request. Moses in Egypt and in the wilderness prayed, Daniel, the three young Hebrews, Elijah, Hannah, David, Jabez, Paul and Silas prayed a definite prevailing prayer.

Prayer is the medium through which man meets with the El-Shaddai God to ask for whatever he desires. It is the most powerful weapon the world has ever known. It is stronger than the best drug on earth to heal all sicknesses. It is an effective weapon to solve all the problems we may have and in meeting every need in the life of man. Importunate means making a repeated and inconvenient request until you triumph over mountains with obstinate refusal to take no for an answer and with passionate faith that would not let go.

The Call to Pray by God

"In Gibeon the LORD appeared to Solomon in a dream by night: and God said, Ask what I shall give thee ... Seek the LORD and his strength, seek his face continually ... Be careful for nothing; but in everything by prayer and supplication with thanksgiving let your requests be made known unto God ... Pray without ceasing" (1 Kings 3:5; 1 Chronicles 16:11; Philippians 4:6; 1 Thessalonians 5:17).

God has called us to pray. We should come to the Him with assurance, persuasion and confidence in what He will definitely do in our lives and pray earnestly to receive our blessings.

The Cause for Importunate Prayer

"Is any sick among you? let him call for the elders of the church; and let them pray over him, anointing him with oil in the name of the Lord: And the prayer of faith shall save the sick, and the Lord shall raise him up; and if he have committed sins, they shall be forgiven him. Confess your faults one to another, and pray one for another, that ye may be healed. The effectual fervent prayer of a righteous man availeth much. Elias was a man subject to like passions as we are, and he prayed earnestly that it might not rain: and it rained not on the earth by the space of three years and six months. And he prayed again, and the heaven gave rain, and the earth brought forth her fruit." (James 5:17-18). The cause for importunate prayer arises:

1. When you are seriously in need of something from God. *"So Hannah rose up after they had eaten in Shiloh, and after they had drunk. Now Eli the priest sat upon a seat by a post of the temple of the Lord. And she was in bitterness of soul, and prayed unto the Lord, and wept sore. And she vowed a vow, and said, O Lord of hosts, if thou wilt indeed look on the affliction of thine handmaid, and remember me, and not forget thine handmaid, but wilt give unto thine handmaid a man child, then I will give him unto the Lord all the days of his life, and there shall no razor come upon his head… Wherefore it came to pass, when the time was come about after Hannah had conceived, that she bare a son, and*

called his name Samuel, saying, Because I have asked him of the Lord" (1 Samuel 1:9-11, 20).

2. When your Christian testimony needs a total change (Genesis 32:24-28).

3. When unbelieving individuals challenge God's promises in your life or ministry.

4. When you need deliverance or healing. *"And at midnight Paul and Silas prayed, and sang praises unto God: and the prisoners heard them. And suddenly there was a great earthquake, so that the foundations of the prison were shaken: and immediately all the doors were opened, and every one's bands were loosed...And lest I should be exalted above measure through the abundance of the revelations, there was given to me a thorn in the flesh, the messenger of Satan to buffet me, lest I should be exalted above measure. For this thing I besought the Lord thrice, that it might depart from me. And he said unto me, My grace is sufficient for thee: for my strength is made perfect in weakness. Most gladly therefore will I rather glory in my infirmities, that the power of Christ may rest upon me."* (Acts 16:25-26; 2 Corinthians 12:7-9).

5. When there's no more hope in a situation (Acts 9:37-41).

6. When you need the power of revival in your life, family and church. *"Now when all the people were baptized, it came to pass, that Jesus also being baptized, and*

praying, the heaven was opened, And the Holy Ghost descended in a bodily shape like a dove upon him, and a voice came from heaven, which said, Thou art my beloved Son; in thee I am well pleased…Then they that gladly received his word were baptized: and the same day there were added unto them about three thousand souls….Howbeit many of them which heard the word believed; and the number of the men was about five thousand" (Luke 3:21-22; Acts 2:41; 4:4).

7. When you are planning for a crusade or special program (Matthew 26:38-44; Acts 13:1-4).

The Cost of Praying Through to Receive Answers

"If I regard iniquity in my heart, the Lord will not hear me… If ye abide in me, and my words abide in you, ye shall ask what ye will, and it shall be done unto you… And Jesus answering saith unto them, Have faith in God. For verily I say unto you, that whosoever shall say unto this mountain, Be thou removed, and be thou cast into the sea; and shall not doubt in his heart, but shall believe that those things which he saith shall come to pass; he shall have whatsoever he saith. Therefore I say unto you, What things soever ye desire, when ye pray, believe that ye receive them, and ye shall have them" (Psalm 66:18; John 15:7; Mark 11:22-24).

- Salvation (Job 27:8-9; Proverbs 15:29; Isaiah 1:15-18)

- Sanctification (Hebrews 12:14; Mark 11:25; Psalm 34:17)
- Praying in the name of Jesus (John 16:23-34; 14:13-14, Matthew 18:20)
- Praying in faith (James 1:6-8; Hebrews 11:1, 6)
- Knowing and standing upon God's promises (Exodus 23:25-26; Joshua 1:5; Psalm 91; Isaiah 40:29-31; Psalm 41: 10,13; Matthew 7:7-11)
- Importunity and perseverance (Genesis 32:26-28; Luke 11:8; 18:1-7)
- Patience (Isaiah 28:16; James 1:3-4).

Catalogue of Answered Prayers in the Bible

There are so many testimonies in the Bible about the ability of God to hear and answer prayers. Here are few of them:

a. Abraham prayed for protection and deliverance for Lot and his family (Genesis 18:20-23; 19:1-22).

b. Barrenness ceased through prayer (Genesis 21:1-2; 25:20-21; 30:22-24; I Samuel 1:20; Judges 13:2-3, 24; 2 Kings 4:14-17; Luke 1:7, 13, 57).

c. Bad luck was removed through prayer (1 Chronicles 20:1-27)

d. Victories through prayer (Isaiah 37:1-38; 2 Chronicles 20:1-27).

e. Sickness healed through prayer (Isaiah 38:1-6; Mark 2:1-12)

f. Dead raised to life through prayer (John 11:1-45)

g. Prosperity through prayer (Psalm 35:27; 118:25).

Our God is mighty to save and strong to deliver. He sets the captives free, provides for the needy and makes a way where there's no way. We have great opportunities in God presence as we approach the throne of mercy in humility and prayer. He will surely supply all good things needed for our well-being.

CHAPTER TWELVE

OUR CALL TO THE GREAT COMMISSION: LIFESTYLE EVANGELISM

"*And Jesus came and spake unto them, saying, All power is given unto me in heaven and in earth. Go ye therefore, and teach all nations, baptizing them in the name of the Father, and of the Son, and of the Holy Ghost: Teaching them to observe all things whatsoever I have commanded you: and, lo, I am with you always, even unto the end of the world. Amen. And that repentance and remission of sins should be preached in his name among all nations, beginning at Jerusalem. And ye are witnesses of these things. And he said unto them, Go ye into all the world, and preach the gospel to every creature. He that believeth and is baptized shall be saved; but he that believeth not shall be damned. Delivering thee from the people, and from the Gentiles, unto whom now I send thee, To open their eyes, and to turn them from darkness to light, and from the power of Satan unto God, that they may receive forgiveness of sins, and inheritance among them which are sanctified by faith that is in me"* (Matthew 28:18-19; Luke 24:47-48; Mark 16:15-16; Acts 26:17-18).

The Great Commission is the most serious, tasking and involving ministry God has given to every believer. This implies that all those who are born again in Christ Jesus must embrace this great and enormous ministry as a call of God upon their lives. The Lord Himself gave the Great Commission to all redeemed souls as a binding mandate to share the gospel of the Lord Jesus Christ with sinners with the aim of leading them to salvation through His vicarious sacrifice. It is a must for us to obey the call of the Great Commission for consolidating our daily victory in Christ, hence making evangelism or soul winning a lifestyle means preaching Christ everywhere and every time. So, lifestyle evangelism is the wisest lifelong duty of the victorious Christian.

Requirements for the Great Commission

As mentioned earlier, every individual who wishes to serve God must, of necessity, meet God's requirements for holy service unto Him. The basic requirements are:

a. **Genuine Salvation**: In 1 Corinthians 15:3-4, *"For I delivered unto you first of all that which I also received, how that Christ died for our sins according to the scriptures; And that he was buried, and that he rose again the third day according to the scriptures."* The Bible makes it clear that the husbandman that laboureth must first be the partaker of his fruit. Therefore, it's important that we have an experimental encounter with the Lord before embarking on preaching assignment to others. *"But unto the wicked God saith, What hast thou to do to declare my statutes, or that thou shouldest take my covenant in thy mouth?"* (Psalm 50:16)

b. **A Transparent and Exemplary Christian Life**: Sanctity must precede service if we must fulfil the Great Commission efficiently. Our lives must be an epistle for others to read. Our lifestyle must not be or seen to be a standing denial of our profession of faith. God is holy, so are His angels and instruments of His service must be holy also. Apostle Peter enjoined us, saying, *"As obedient children, not fashioning yourselves according to the former lusts in your ignorance: But as he which hath called you is holy, so be ye holy in all manner of conversation; Because it is written, Be ye holy; for I am holy."* (I Peter 1:14-15). *"Depart ye, depart ye, go ye out from thence, touch no unclean thing; go ye out of the midst of her; be ye clean, that bear the vessels of the Lord… Let no man despise thy youth; but be thou an example of* *the believers, in word, in conversation, in charity, in spirit, in faith, in purity."* (Isaiah 52:11; I Timothy 4:12).

c. **Vision and Compassion:** The missionary vision must begin with the vision of God's love and compassion. *"Where there is no vision, the people perish: but he that keepeth the law, happy is he... But when he saw the multitudes, he was moved with compassion on them, because they fainted, and were scattered abroad, as sheep having no shepherd. Then saith he unto his disciples, The harvest truly is plenteous, but the labourers are few; Pray ye therefore the Lord of the harvest, that he will send forth labourers into his harvest"* (Proverbs 29:18; Mathew 9:36-38).

d. **Knowledge of God's Word:** The challenge we should take upon ourselves is to give due diligence to the study of God's Word daily for personal development and growth. *"Therefore, my people are gone into captivity, because they have no knowledge: and their honourable men are famished, and their multitude dried up with thirst... Study to shew thyself approved unto God, a workman that needeth not to be ashamed, rightly dividing the word of truth"* (Isaiah 5:13; 2 Timothy 2:15).

E. **Tactfulness**: The Great Commission is the most difficult task to do. It is more difficult than preaching because it involves confrontational battle with the devil. Hence tact and wisdom are required to be an effective soul winner. *"The fruit of the righteous is a tree of life; and he that winneth souls is wise"* (Proverbs 11:30). *"No man can enter into a strong man's house, and spoil his goods, except he will first bind the strong man; and then he will spoil his house."* Mark 3:27

f. **Being a Man of Prayer:** To advance God's work, we must employ the weapons of prayer continually. *"And he spake a parable unto them to this end, that men ought always to pray, and not to faint; Finally, my brethren, be strong in the Lord, and in the power of his might"* (Luke 18:1; Ephesians 6:10).

g. **Operating as a Man of Faith:** Without faith, our service to God cannot be pleasing unto Him. *"Above all, taking the shield of faith, wherewith ye shall be able to quench all the fiery darts of the wicked."* (Ephesians 6:16).

h. **Infilling with the Holy Ghost:** The Holy Spirit Divine is the power behind the success of the early Church's proclamation of the Gospel. The boldness and exploits of Peter who had earlier denied Jesus became possible by the empowering of the Holy Spirit when he stood in the very place where Jesus had been condemned and boldly proclaimed Him. *"Now when they heard this, they were pricked in their heart, and said unto Peter and to the rest of the apostles, Men and brethren, what shall we do? Then Peter, filled with the Holy Ghost, said unto them, Ye rulers of* the people, and elders of Israel... And when they had prayed, the place was shaken where they were assembled together; and they were all filled with the Holy Ghost, and they spake the word of God with boldness"* (Acts 2:37; 4:8,31).

Reasons for Obeying the Great Commission

"For God so loved the world, that he gave his only begotten Son, that whosoever believeth in him should not perish, but have everlasting life...My sheep hear my voice, and I know them, and they follow me: And I give unto them eternal life; and they shall never perish, neither shall any man pluck them out of my hand...Jesus saith unto them, My meat is to do the will of him that sent me, and to finish his work. Say not ye, There are yet four months, and then cometh harvest? behold, I say unto you, Lift up your eyes, and look on the fields; for they are white already to harvest... Then Peter and the other apostles answered and said, We ought to obey God rather than men" (John 3:16; 10:27-28; 4:34, 35; Acts 5:29).

Our Lord Jesus Christ is our perfect example of obedience. *"For even hereunto were ye called: because Christ also suffered for us, leaving us an example, that ye should follow his steps"* (1 Peter 2:21). We must follow His example. He obeyed His Father's command. We are to obey Him by declaring to the whole world that He is the Saviour. Other reasons we have to obey the Great Commission are that:

1. It is the heart-beat of God.
2. It determines the present and future condition and destiny of sinners.
3. The harvest is plenteous.
4. Time is short.
5. God's judgement is sure.
6. Satan is more aggressive than ever to launch a final attack on men's souls.

The commandments of the Lord are meant to be obeyed. The Great Commission is urgent and should be speedily executed because many souls are dying and going into Christless eternity. If we are faithful and obedient, many souls will be won into the kingdom of God.

Reward of Obedience to the Great Commission

"And they that be wise shall shine as the brightness of the firmament; and they that turn many to righteousness as the stars for ever and ever... His lord said unto him, Well done, good and faithful servant; thou hast been faithful over a few things, I will make thee ruler over many things: enter thou into the joy of thy lord... And when the chief Shepherd shall appear, ye shall receive a crown of glory that fadeth not away... Jesus answered and said unto him, If a man love me, he will keep my words: and my Father will love him, and we will come unto him, and

make our abode with him" (Daniel 12:3; Matthew 25:23; 1 Peter 5:4; John 14:23).

Eternal rewards await all the faithful and obedient disciples of Christ. There can be no other profitable venture than to engage in the business of soul winning. It gladdens the heart of Almighty God when a soul is won into the Kingdom of God. Angels rejoice and all Heaven is thrown into jubilation God. *"I say unto you, that likewise joy shall be in heaven over one sinner that repenteth, more than over ninety and nine just persons, which need no repentance"* (Luke 15:7).

CHAPTER THIRTEEN

SPIRITUAL GROWTH AND DEVELOPMENT

"And God blessed them, and God said unto them, Be fruitful, and multiply, and replenish the earth, and subdue it: and have dominion over the fish of the sea, and over the fowl of the air, and over every living thing that moveth upon the earth... And the child grew, and waxed strong in spirit, filled with wisdom: and the grace of God was upon him... But grow in grace, and in the knowledge of our Lord and Saviour Jesus Christ. To him be glory both now and forever. Amen" (Genesis 1:28; Luke 2:40; 2 Peter 3:18).

Growth is an integral characteristic of living organisms and the absence of it indicates the presence of a disease. He who stops growing starts decaying says a popular maxim. The desire for growth is an inborn tendency in man. It is God's ordained program and plan for every man to grow. The command to be fruitful and multiply can only be possible when there is growth. Ironically, growth in every area of life, except spiritual growth, is one of the most passionate pursuits in the world today. It is said that an active and expressible spirituality is one that sets humanity apart from the rest of the living things. From the book, *A Deeper Look at What the Bible Says about Spiritual Growth*, it was stated that: "Humans are innately spiritual, and our unique awareness of spirituality is something that marks humanity as distinct."

Spiritual growth means waxing strong in the spirit, reaching forth beyond: *"That Christ may dwell in your hearts by faith; that ye, being rooted and grounded in love, May be able to comprehend with all saints what is the breadth, and length, and depth, and height; And to know the love of Christ, which passeth knowledge, that ye might be filled with all the fulness of God"* (Ephesians 3:17-19). Attaining God's fullness: *"Till we all come in the unity of the faith, and of the knowledge of the Son of God, unto a perfect man, unto the measure of the stature of the fulness of Christ"* (Ephesians 4:13). Large heartedness: *"O ye Corinthians, our mouth is open unto you, our heart is enlarged… And God gave Solomon wisdom and understanding exceeding much, and largeness of heart, even as the sand that is on the sea shore"* (2 Corinthians 6:11; 1 Kings 4:29). Character building and attitudinal change: *"And beside this, giving all diligence, add to your faith virtue; and to virtue knowledge; And to knowledge temperance; and to temperance patience; and to patience godliness; And to godliness brotherly kindness; and to brotherly kindness charity. For if these things be in you, and abound, they make you that ye shall neither be barren nor unfruitful in the knowledge of our Lord Jesus Christ. But he that lacketh these things is blind, and cannot see afar off, and hath forgotten that he was purged from his old sins. Wherefore the rather, brethren, give diligence to make your calling and election sure: for if ye do these things, ye shall never fall"* (2 Peter 1:5-10).

Growth goes beyond mere wishes; it is God that gives growth. It must be worked out through personal commitment and consecration though, it is not in the power or might of a mortal man to grow on his own, *"Abide in me, and I in you. As the branch cannot bear fruit of itself, except it abide in the vine; no more can ye, except ye abide in me"* (John 15:4); yet man has a crucial role to play in the process.

Apostle Paul, while acknowledging and attributing his ministerial success to the grace of God, yet did not take the grace in vain but laboured more abundantly than others. Preservation by grace with which we are saved until the end requires growing in that grace.

Unfortunately, many Christians are not growing as expected. This is evidenced by the lifestyle of many professing church members today. *"For when for the time ye ought to be teachers, ye have need that one teach you again which be the first principles of the oracles of God; and are become such as have need of milk, and not of strong meat. For every one that useth milk is unskilful in the word of righteousness: for he is a babe. But strong meat belongeth to them that are of full age, even those who by reason of use have their senses exercised to discern both good and evil…They profess that they know God; but in works they deny him, being abominable, and disobedient, and unto every good work reprobate…And I, brethren, could not speak unto you as unto spiritual, but as unto carnal, even as unto babes in Christ. I have fed you with milk, and not with meat: for hitherto ye were not able to bear it, neither yet now are ye able. For ye are yet carnal: for whereas there is among you envying, and strife, and divisions, are ye not carnal, and walk as men? For while one saith, I am of Paul; and another, I am of Apollos; are ye not carnal?"* (Hebrews 5:12-14; Titus 1:16; 1 Corinthians 3:1-4). Spiritual growth reflects as maturity displayed spiritually, emotionally, mentally, socially and verbally.

Purpose of Spiritual Growth

Immediate after salvation, every believer is expected to grow to become like Christ. The ultimate goal of conversion is to regain the lost image of God. This is now

Spiritual Growth and Development

made possible through Jesus Christ Who is the express image of the Father.

"Who being the brightness of his glory, and the express image of his person, and upholding all things by the word of his power, when he had by himself purged our sins, sat down on the right hand of the Majesty on high....Wherefore seeing we also are compassed about with so great a cloud of witnesses, let us lay aside every weight, and the sin which doth so easily beset us, and let us run with patience the race that is set before us, Looking unto Jesus the author and finisher of our faith; who for the joy that was set before him endured the cross, despising the shame, and is set down at the right hand of the throne of God...Till we all come unto the measure and the stature of the fulness of Christ ((Hebrews 1:3; 12:1-2; Ephesians 4:13).

Constantly focusing on Jesus will enhance our stability to avoid vulnerability to falsehood and deception of the enemy. Hence, it should be our priority and purpose in life. There should be an intense and unquenchable thirst for God in the heart as David had, *"As the hart panteth after the water brooks, so panteth my soul after thee, O God… O God, thou art my God; early will I seek thee: my soul thirsteth for thee, my flesh longeth for thee in a dry and thirsty land, where no water is; To see thy power and thy glory, so as I have seen thee in the sanctuary. Because thy lovingkindness is better than life, my lips shall praise thee"* (Psalm 42:1; 63:1-3). Apostle Paul, in his epistle to young Timothy, charged him to give priority to the Word for particular purposes which include:

1. To be well equipped as a minister rightly dividing the word of truth.
2. To know God's mind, desire and demand from Him and His laity.
3. To properly feed the flock
4. To build conviction in his hearers
5. To earnestly contend for the Faith
6. To convincingly and courageously declare the truth and
7. To make full proof of the ministry.

Process of Spiritual Growth

"Can the rush grow up without mire? can the flag grow without water? Blessed is the man that walketh not in the counsel of the ungodly, nor standeth in the way of sinners, nor sitteth in the seat of the scornful. But his delight is in the law of the Lord; and in his law doth he meditate day and night. And he shall be like a tree planted by the rivers of water, that bringeth forth his fruit in his season; his leaf also shall not wither; and whatsoever he

doeth shall prosper...This book of the law shall not depart out of thy mouth; but thou shalt meditate therein day and night, that thou mayest observe to do according to all that is written therein: for then thou shalt make thy way prosperous, and then thou shalt have good success... thou hast planted them, yea, they have taken root: they grow, yea, they bring forth fruit: thou art near in their mouth, and far from their reins" (Job 8:11; Psalm 1:1-3; Joshua 1:8; Jeremiah 12:2).

The process of spiritual growth starts at conversion when a sinner who is dead in sin and trespasses is quickened by the Spirit of God to be alive spiritually. In other words, sinners and backsliders cannot grow spiritually because only living things grow, except they repent and get converted. Hence the stages of growth as:

1. Infants: newborn babies are fed with milk (Hebrews 5:13).

2. Little children: those able to walk and talk (1 John 2:12, 13c).

3. Young men: the strong and agile for Lord and able to withstand the enemy (1 John 2:13b, 14b).

4. Fathers: Spiritual parents and leaders who are full of age for discernment (1 John 2:13a; Hebrews 5:14).

God's will is that every believer should move accordingly from the first stage to the last one. Therefore, man must not only desire to grow but be also ready to pay the price. If a believer would grow in the Lord, the following principles are essentials:

a. Focused desire - "*Through desire a man, having separated himself, seeketh and intermeddleth with all wisdom*" (Proverbs 18:1). Without desire, nothing meaningful can be achieved. Desire is the propelling force to drive the believer. "Winners in life think constantly in terms of I can, I will, and I am. Losers, on the other hand, concentrate their waking thought on what they should have or would have done or what they can't do" Denis Waitley. "Whatever the mind of man can conceive and believe, it can achieve. Thoughts are things! And powerful things at that, when mixed with definiteness of purpose, and burning desire, can be translated into riches" - Napoleon Hill. The same thing applies to spiritual growth.

b. Frequent reading and feeding on the word of God (Joshua 1:8; 1 Peter 2:2; 3:8): *Can the rush grow up without mire? Can the flag grow without water?* (Job 8:11). As God's word is fuel for the refiner's sanctifying fire, so also is water for the planted tree's growth and a rock-solid foundation for the builder to build. Reading without real meditation will yield little or no result just like undigested food to the body. It is the meditation that strengthens the spirit of man as digested food strengthens the natural body.

c. Fervent and regular life of praying with fasting (when necessary). *"And he spake a parable unto them to this end, that men ought always to pray, and not to faint"* (Luke 18:1). No believer can grow beyond his prayer life. A life of prayer and devotion has remained the hallmark of God's children in all ages. Scriptural fasting strengthens the spiritual life and ensures steady growth of the believer. *"Howbeit this kind goeth not out but by prayer and fasting."* (Matthew 17:21)

d. Fruitful soul-winning. *"The fruit of the righteous is a tree of life; and he that winneth souls is wise...Herein is my Father glorified, that ye bear much fruit; so shall ye be my disciples"* (Proverbs 11:30; John 15: 8). Commitment to the Great Commission will eventually lead to the growth and development of the spiritual life.

e. Fellowship with God's people. *"Not forsaking the assembling of ourselves together, as the manner of some is; but exhorting one another: and so much the more, as ye see the day approaching"* (Hebrews 10:25). Fellowship is spending time and doing things with others who love Christ. *"Iron sharpeneth iron; so a man sharpeneth the countenance of his friend."* (Proverbs 27:17). The church community is meant to be a spiritual family united together to promote growth and development. When the church gathers, members inspire one another to grow deeper with God through corporate worship, reading and hearing God's word and prayers. *"That which we have seen and heard declare we unto you, that ye also may have fellowship with us: and truly our fellowship is with the Father, and with his Son Jesus Christ."* (1 John 1:3)

f. Faithful daily Christian living. *"I have given them thy word; and the world hath hated them, because they are not of the world, even as I am not of the world"* (John 17:14). As salt and light of the world, the believer radiates the beauty of Christ in his day-to-day living in the world and stands unpolluted with the system of the world. *"Pure religion and undefiled before God and the Father is this, To visit the fatherless and widows in their affliction, and to keep himself unspotted from the world."* (James 1:27)

Blessings of Spiritual Growth

"Then he answered and spake unto me, saying, This is the word of the Lord unto Zerubbabel, saying, Not by might, nor by power, but by my spirit, saith the Lord of hosts… That our sons may be as plants grown up in their youth; that our daughters may be as corner stones, polished after the similitude of a palace… I will be as the dew unto Israel: he shall grow as the lily, and cast forth his roots as Lebanon" (Zechariah 4:6; Psalm 144:12; Hosea 14:5).

Whatever God desires, He has power to accomplish. He has promised, "*The righteous shall flourish like the palm tree: he shall grow like a cedar in Lebanon*" (Psalm 92:12).

It is possible for those who are currently dried or experiencing stunted growth to experience spiritual growth. Every dry borne shall rise again as the Lord commanded it (Ezekiel 37:1-10). These blessings include:

a. Spiritual refreshing. (Psalm 1:3; Acts 3:19)

b. Fruitfulness. (John 15:6)

c. Fulfilment in life and satisfaction. (Psalm 91:16)

CHAPTER FOURTEEN

RIDING ON THE STORMS OF LIFE

"And the same day, when the even was come, he saith unto them, Let us pass over unto the other side. And when they had sent away the multitude, they took him even as he was in the ship. And there were also with him other little ships. And there arose a great storm of wind, and the waves beat into the ship, so that it was now full. And he was in the hinder part of the ship, asleep on a pillow: and they awake him, and say unto him, Master, carest thou not that we perish? And he arose, and rebuked the wind, and said unto the sea, Peace, be still. And the wind ceased, and there was a great calm. And he said unto them, why are ye so fearful? how is it that ye have no faith?" (Mark 4:35-40).

Christ's disciples were on board a ship travelling to the other side of the lake. It wasn't just a jolly fun ride. They have a divine purpose. They were on a mission and the Lord was on the trip. Yet while on the high sea, a great tempest arose *"And, behold, there arose a great tempest in the sea, insomuch that the ship was covered with the waves: but he was asleep"* (Matthew 8:24).

The storm stirred the sea into angry billows splashing against and into the ship threatening to sink it. In fear, distress and desperation, the Apostles yelled and charged the Lord, *"Carest thou not that we perish?"* For while the sea raged, the wind howled and the billows rolled the Lord lay nestled on a pillow having a good sleep! He arose and calmed the storm with a three-word command, *"Peace, be still."*

This incident, narrated by the three synoptic gospels (Matthew 8:23-27; Mark 4:35-40; Luke 8:22-25) pictures the natural reactions of people in great trouble especially when it seems the Lord doesn't care; or He appears too slow to act and command a solution. Whatever the situation, *"And there arose a great storm of wind,"* when the Lord rebuked the wind, *"there was a great calm."*

The great storm resulted in a great calm. Fresh conflicts might arise so severe that they challenge the validity of our relationship with the Lord and stretch out our faith to its limit, even tempting us to ask the Lord in desperation "*Carest thou not that we perish?*"

Storms are normal negative developments in life and everyone will have their own share. Never think you aren't ever going to have a problem (a storm) in your life time. "*Man that is born of a woman is of few days and full of trouble... Let the redeemed of the Lord say so, whom he hath redeemed from the hand of the enemy; And gathered them out of the lands, from the east, and from the west, from the north, and from the south. They wandered in the wilderness in a solitary way; they found no city to dwell in. Hungry and thirsty, their soul fainted in them*" (Job 14:1; Psalm 107:1-6).

The Saviour never promised us candy life. While on this earth no man can enjoy insulation against difficulties, problems and negative challenges. It doesn't matter who are sinners cry; saints, too, sigh. God's word doesn't guarantee anyone the immunity to pain and grief. God has fixed it that nature should have both smooth sail and rough times and that all men should experience both. "*While the earth remaineth, seedtime and harvest, and cold and heat, and summer and winter, and day and night shall not cease*" (Genesis 8:22).

The comfort of the Scripture is that the Saviour won't abandon His people who are going through any kind of storm. "*But now thus saith the Lord that created thee, O Jacob,* and he that formed thee, O Israel, Fear not: for I have redeemed thee, I have called thee by thy name; thou art mine. When thou passest through the waters, I will be with thee; and through the rivers, they shall not overflow thee: when thou walkest through the fire, thou shalt not be burned; neither shall the flame kindle upon thee"* (Isaiah 43:1-2).

He will arise to their prayers for help, still the wind and create a safe passage. Say a loud Amen! Therefore, we need not despair though the storms arise in our way and our road be rough. If the Saviour is on board with us, we can rely on His power, call upon His great name and decree a calm.

Catalogue of Life's Storms

A life's storm is any negative happening or situation that hinders progress in one's desired area of life and disturbs one's total well-being. It threatens to abort a mission, annul a purpose and make the future look bleak. Looking at the Scriptures, this definition fits the recorded experiences of certain saints, backsliders and sinners. Life's storms include but are not limited to:

a. **Persecution and Oppression.** *"Blessed are ye, when men shall hate you, and when they shall separate you from their company, and shall reproach you, and cast out your name as evil, for the Son of man's sake...Who shall separate us from the love of Christ? shall tribulation, or distress, or persecution, or* *famine, or nakedness, or peril, or sword?... Yea, and all that will live godly in Christ Jesus shall suffer persecution"* (Luke 6:22; Romans 8:35; 2 Timothy 3:12).

Persecutions are the common experience of all believers. Joseph was hated and sold into slavery by his brethren for relating his God-given dreams. Jeremiah, Elijah, Elisha and other prophets suffered for upholding the scepter of righteousness as did Shadrach, Meshach, Abednego and Daniel for their stand in worshipping the only true God. The Lord Jesus Christ was vehemently persecuted by the religionists of His day.

The apostolic and church fathers suffered many persecutions. This is because the religious society hated and still hates anyone who walks contrary to the 'traditions' of the elders to please the Lord. Hence, the world will rage if anyone breaks away from their helpless traditions and stands for the truth.

"And when they had brought them, they set them before the council: and the high priest asked them, Saying, Did not we straitly command you that ye should not teach in this name? und, behold, ye have filled Jerusalem with your doctrine, and intend to bring this man's blood upon us. Then Peter and the other apostles answered and said, We ought to obey God rather than men...And to him they agreed: and when they had called the apostles, and beaten them, they commanded that they

should not speak in the name of Jesus, and let them go." (Acts 5:27-29, 40).

Every believer must take his stand for the Lord and his love, peace, joy and faith during persecution must ramain unshakable. There is a great heavenly reward for those who endure to the end. They shall be rewarded for every pain and suffering they passed through for Christ's sake. The overcomers will reign with Christ in glory.

b. **Blocked Advancement and Privileges**. *"Wherefore we would have come unto you, even I Paul, once and again; but Satan hindered us...For which cause also I have been much hindered from coming to you."* (1 Thessalonians 2:18; Romans 15:22). Hindrances are as a result of satanic activities and that of his demons whose ways are devious, evil, implacable, insidious, corrupt, immoral and crafty. They oppose and persecute men and women of God with the aim of derailing them to lose focus on God's perfect plan for them.

This has been happening down through all the ages by closing doors of opportunities in which misunderstandings throw mission work into confusion. Jannes and Jambres withstood Moses, imitating his wonders by their demonic power of enchantments - an ingenious imitation of Romanism to constitute hindrances to the Gospel. *"Now as Jannes and Jambres withstood Moses, so do these also resist the truth: men of corrupt minds, reprobate concerning the faith* "(2 Timothy 3:8).

Achan hindered Israel's advancement; so also, is the ministry of Achan in the Church as a traitor in the camp of God's army today. *"And Achan answered Joshua, and said, Indeed I have sinned against the Lord God of Israel, and thus and thus have I done: When I saw among the spoils a goodly Babylonish garment, and two hundred shekels of silver, and a wedge of gold of fifty shekels weight, then I coveted them, and took them; and, behold, they are hid in the earth in the midst of my tent, and the silver under it."* (Joshua 7:20-21).

Herod and the Jews sought to hinder the New Testament Church from marching forward with all sorts of persecutions and tribulation and yet, the gate of hell could not prevail against the will of God. *"Now about that time Herod the king stretched forth his hands to vex certain of the church. And he killed James the brother of John with the sword. And because he saw it pleased the Jews, he proceeded further to take Peter also. (Then were the days of unleavened bread.) And when he had apprehended him, he put him in prison, and delivered him to four quaternions of soldiers to keep him; intending after Easter to bring him forth to the people...And the angel said unto him, Gird thyself, and bind on thy sandals. And so he did. And he saith unto him, Cast thy garment about thee, and follow me... And when Peter was come to himself, he said, Now I know of a surety, that the Lord hath sent his angel, and hath delivered me out of the hand of Herod, and from all the expectation of the people of the Jews"* (Acts 12:1-4, 8, 11). The good news is that, Christ has defeated satan for us on the cross of Calvary. As we resist him steadfastly in prayers, he will surely flee from us; and every stronghold, roadblock and iron bar to your advancement and success spiritually and physically can be pulled down by a prayer of faith.

c. **Sudden or Prolonged Sickness.** *"So went Satan forth from the presence of the Lord, and smote Job with sore boils from the sole of his foot unto his crown. And he took him a potsherd to scrape himself withal; and he sat down among the ashes… And, behold, there was a woman which had a spirit of infirmity eighteen years, and was bowed together, and could in no wise lift up herself. And when Jesus saw her, he called her to him, and said unto her, Woman, thou art loosed from thine infirmity. And he laid his hands on her: and immediately she was made straight, and glorified God…And ought not this woman, being a daughter of Abraham, whom Satan hath bound, lo, these eighteen years, be loosed from this bond on the sabbath day?"* (Job 2:7-8; Luke 13:11-13, 16).

The miracle of healing and remaining healthy is the children's bread in the Kingdom - an act of God's divine grace. Jesus not only bore our sins, but He also bore our sickness and diseases. He became our sickness-Bearer in exactly the same way He became our sin-Bearer. Christ was scourged and striped for our healing and nailed to the cross for our sins. *"But he was wounded for our transgressions, he was bruised for our iniquities: the chastisement of our peace was upon him; and with his stripes we are healed"* (Isaiah 53:5).

By God's divine arrangement, divine healing and health, like salvation and redemption, sanctification and justification, healing and health have remained the right of every child of God. As rightly stated in the scriptures, *"Christ hath redeemed us from the curse of the law"* including sicknesses, diseases, and infirmities found in people's lives today. *"Who his own self bare our sins in his own body on the tree, that we, being dead to sins, should live unto righteousness: by whose stripes ye were healed"* (1 Peter 2:24). For a believer to enjoy the divine benefits of our redemption, he must obey the totality of God's holy word. It then goes without saying that, *"…the curse causeless shall not come"* (Proverbs 26:2).

In most cases, infirmities come as a consequence of disobeying God's word. *"And said, If thou wilt diligently hearken to the voice of the LORD thy God, and wilt do that which is right in his sight, and wilt give ear to his commandments, and keep all his statutes, I will put none of these diseases upon thee, which I have brought upon the Egyptians: for I am the LORD that healeth thee"* (Exodus 15:26).

d. **Marriage and Family Problems.** *"Marriage is honourable in all, and the bed undefiled: but whoremongers and adulterers God will judge...And it came to pass after this, that Absalom the son of David had a fair sister, whose name was Tamar; and Amnon the son of David loved her. And Amnon was so vexed, that he fell sick for his sister Tamar; for she was a virgin; and Amnon thought it hard for him to do anything to her."* (Hebrews 13:4; 2 Samuel 13:1-2, 10-14, 19-22, 28-29). **Marriage is a divine institution ordained by God to fulfil a divine purpose**. Before the institution of marriage, God made necessary preparation in order for the man to enjoy the best. If you are in Christ Jesus today, then you are not alone. The Architect of marriage is on your side. And with Him, "all things are possible." Victory is sure for you in Jesus name! The fact that family problems are almost inevitable is enough reason to make proper preparation for a Godly marriage within God's plan, purpose and provision right from the beginning. (Genesis 2:18, 20, 22, 24; Matthew 19:4-5; Ephesians 5:31)

For the single believer

"Better is the end of a thing than the beginning thereof: and the patient in spirit is better than the proud in spirit. Can two walks together, except they be agreed? House and riches are the inheritance of fathers: and a prudent wife is from the Lord" (Ecclesiastes 7:8; Amos 3:3; Proverbs 19:14).

One of the causes of unhappy homes and the painful union is the unequal yoke. If a child of God marries a child of the devil, he is certain to have troubles with his father-in-law. Also, when a Christian man marries a lady who has some connection with the mermaid spirit, he will have troubles with his mother-in-law. The unequal yoke causes many problems to the flesh and often leads to a lifetime of painful consequences. The result may be hell on earth and a loss of Heaven in eternity.

It is important not to belittle the selection process. Don't take the decision lightly. Don't rationalize in your mind what you know in your heart will not be spiritually and eternally beneficial. Let God have His way, let God choose for you through prayers and be led by His Spirit.

e. **Barrenness in Marriage**

"*And God blessed them, and God said unto them, Be fruitful, and multiply, and replenish the earth, and subdue it: and have dominion over the fish of the sea, and over the fowl of the air, and over every living thing that moveth upon the earth…There shall nothing cast their young, nor be barren, in thy land: the number of thy days I will fulfil…Thou shalt be blessed above all people: there shall not be male or female barren among you, or among your cattle*" (Genesis 1:28; Exodus 23:26; Deuteronomy 7:14). These promises are nothing but divine favour and providential care of the Almighty God.

Barrenness in marriage is never the will of God for the couple. Scientifically, one of the major characteristics of living things is reproduction; man is naturally endowed by his Creator to reproduce. Wherever and whenever unfruitfulness is experienced, the Bible reveals that, *"An enemy has done this"* (Matthew 13:28).

Therefore, both husband and wife must be involved in violent prayers of faith. Prayer times which are organized for such people are often tireless, very aggressive, serious, physically and emotionally draining until something happens.

The only woman on record in the Bible who remained barren until death was Michal, Saul's daughter, because she despised the anointed King David. *"And David danced before the Lord with all his might; and David was girded with a linen ephod... And as the ark of the Lord came into the city of David, Michal Saul's daughter looked through a window, and saw king David leaping and dancing before the Lord; and she despised him in her heart...* ***Then David returned to bless his household. And Michal the daughter of Saul came out to meet David, and said, How glorious was the king of Israel to day, who uncovered himself to day in the eyes of the handmaids of his servants, as one of the vain fellows shamelessly uncovereth himself! And David said unto Michal, It was before the Lord, which chose me before thy father, and before all his house, to appoint me ruler over*** *the people of the Lord, over Israel: therefore will I play before the Lord. And I will yet be more vile than thus, and will be base in mine own sight: and of the maidservants which thou hast spoken of, of them shall I be had in honour. Therefore Michal the daughter of Saul had no child unto the day of her death"* (2 Samuel 6:14, 16, 20-23).

However, barren women were healed in answer to prayer several times in the Bible. Remember, God is not partial. If you seek His face in prayer of faith, He will surely answer your prayer also. As He did for Sarah, Rebekah, Rachel, Hannah and Elizabeth, yours is the next in Jesus' name!

f. **Famine and Poverty**

"And there was a famine in the land: and Abram went down into Egypt to sojourn there; for the famine was grievous in the land...And there was a famine in the land, beside the first famine that was in the days of Abraham. And Isaac went unto Abimelech king of the Philistines unto Gerar" (Genesis 12:10; 26:1). But God promised to bless us spiritually and physically. *"Blessed be the God and Father of our Lord Jesus Christ, who hath blessed us with all spiritual blessings in heavenly places in Christ"* (Ephesians 1:3). The Lord is going to shower blessings upon everyone from the heavenly places as He has blessed us already.

Salvation, restoration, holiness, grace, healing, power, authority are available in God's presence every moment. In heavenly places with Christ, we have access to things pertaining to life and godliness. Therefore, suffering, enemies, lack and problems are under our feet. *"He sent his word, and healed them, and delivered them from their destructions" (Psalms 107:20).*

The moment the word of God enters into your life, healing, deliverance and divine provisions will accompany it too. *"The young lions do lack, and suffer hunger: but they that seek the LORD shall not want any good thing…But my God shall supply all your need according to his riches in glory by Christ Jesus"* (Psalm 34:10; Philippians 4:19).

g. **Satanic Attacks**
"So went Satan forth from the presence of the Lord, and smote Job with sore boils from the sole of his foot unto his crown. And he took him a potsherd to scrape himself withal; and he sat down among the ashes … And he was teaching in one of the synagogues on the sabbath. And, behold, there was a woman which had a spirit of infirmity eighteen years, and was bowed together, and could in no wise lift up herself. And when Jesus saw her, he called her to him, and said unto her, Woman, thou art loosed from thine infirmity. And he laid his hands on her: and immediately she was made straight, and glorified

God. And the ruler of the synagogue answered with indignation, because that Jesus had healed on the sabbath day, and said unto the people, There are six days in which men ought to work: in them therefore come and be healed, and not on the sabbath day. The Lord then answered him, and said, Thou hypocrite, doth not each one of you on the sabbath loose his ox or his ass from the stall, and lead him away to watering? And ought not this woman, being a daughter of Abraham, whom Satan hath bound, lo, these eighteen years, be loosed from this bond on the sabbath day?" (Job 2:7-8; Luke 13:10-16).

Satan is looking frantically for any opportunity to unleash sickness at Christians and create very bad situations for them. He has his agents demons, witches and wizard - around to execute his evil onslaughts.

Unfortunately, many people are unaware of satan's plan for them. Thus, they stroll into his net through fellowship with his agents (false prophets and teachers) and by the acquisition of cursed items or fetishes. *"Up, sanctify the people, and say, Sanctify yourselves against to morrow: for thus saith the Lord God of Israel, There is an accursed thing in the midst of thee, O Israel: thou canst not stand before thine enemies, until ye take away the accursed thing from among you... And Achan answered Joshua, and said, Indeed I have sinned against the Lord God of Israel, and thus and thus have I done: When I saw among the spoils a goodly Babylonish* garment, and two hundred shekels of silver, and a wedge of gold of fifty shekels weight, then I coveted them, and took them; and, behold, they are hid in the earth in the midst of my tent, and the silver under it." (Joshua 7:13, 20-21).

Many people have brought hardship unto themselves through the possession of items dedicated to idols. There are those who do business with the devil and get their dividends from him in form of sicknesses and other terrible experiences.

Conquering Life's Storms

"Such as sit in darkness and in the shadow of death, being bound in affliction and iron; Because they rebelled against the words of God, and contemned the counsel of the most High: Therefore he brought down their heart with labour; they fell down, and there was none to help. Then they cried unto the Lord in their trouble, and he saved them out of their distresses. He brought them out of darkness and the shadow of death, and brake their bands in sunder... Fools because of their transgression, and because of their iniquities, are afflicted. Their soul abhorreth all manner of meat; and they draw near unto the gates of death. Then they cry unto the Lord in their trouble, and he saveth them out of their distresses. He sent his word, and healed them, and delivered them from their destructions... Be sober, be vigilant; because your adversary the devil, as a roaring lion, walketh about,

seeking whom he may devour: Whom resist stedfast in the faith, knowing that the same afflictions are accomplished in your brethren that are in the world... Submit yourselves therefore to God. Resist the devil, and he will flee from you" (Psalm 107:10-14, 17-20; 1Peter 5:5-8; James 4:7).

It's very certain that storms of life would arise, but we can conquer the storms and go fulfilling the will and purpose of God for our lives. Our victory over the storms of life, however, comes in a process. You need to examine yourself and do the following:

1. Conduct a Search First, we should ascertain that the storms aren't products of our own sins or divine punishment for acts of rebellion. If they are, then we own up, confess, repent and pray for pardon in Jesus' name.

"Examine yourselves, whether ye be in the faith; prove your own selves. Know ye not your own selves, how that Jesus Christ is in you, except ye be reprobates?...Search me, O God, and know my heart: try me, and know my thoughts: And see if there be any wicked way in me, and lead me in the way everlasting... But let none of you suffer as a murderer, or as a thief, or as an evildoer, or as a busybody in other men's matters" (2 Corinthians 13:5; Psalm 139:23-24; 1 Peter 4:15).

2. Cry to the Saviour Then we should pray with faith, sincerely, fervently and persistently until the Lord arises and still the storms. *"And his disciples came to him, and awoke him, saying, Lord, save us: we perish... The righteous cry, and the Lord heareth, and delivereth them out of all their troubles... Many are the afflictions of the righteous: but the Lord delivereth him out of them all"* (Matthew 8:25; Psalm 34:17, 19).

3. Contest against Satan We shouldn't allow Satan to roam in our lives. Whenever we see him at work we should arise, stop his activities, chase him and lock him out. *"Submit yourselves therefore to God. Resist the devil, and he will flee from you"* (James 4:7).

4. Confess your Success When the weather becomes clear and calm and life bloom again, we shouldn't forget to share our testimonies, and praise the name and power of the Lord who on our behalf fought the devil and tame the sea. *"And he said unto them, Where is your faith? And they being afraid wondered, saying one to another, What manner of man is this! for he commandeth even the winds and water, and they obey him"* (Luke 8:25).

5. Continue in Service We shouldn't chicken out of our loyalty to Christ and His service because of storms. Those who drifted with the tide would end up in the belly of the sea. The only way of surviving every storm of life is to abide in the Lord and ensure He's ever on board with us.

"Abide in me, and I in you. As the branch cannot bear fruit of

itself, except it abide in the vine; no more can ye, except ye abide in me. I am the vine, ye are the branches: He that abideth in me, and I in him, the same bringeth forth much fruit: for without me ye can do nothing. If a man abide not in me, he is cast forth as a branch, and is withered; and men gather them, and cast them into the fire, and they are burned. If ye abide in me, and my words abide in you, ye shall ask what ye will, and it shall be done unto you" (John 15:4-7).

CHAPTER FIFTEEN

DISCOVERING YOUR PROPHETIC DESTINY

"But we speak the wisdom of God in a mystery, even the hidden wisdom, which God ordained before the world unto our glory: Which none of the princes of this world knew: for had they known it, they would not have crucified the Lord of glory. But as it is written, Eye hath not seen, nor ear heard, neither have entered into the heart of man, the things which God hath prepared for them that love him... Then said I, Lo, I come (in the volume of the book it is written of me,) to do thy will, O God... And he trembling and astonished said, Lord, what wilt thou have me to do? And the Lord said unto him, Arise, and go into the city, and it shall be told thee what thou must do" (1 Corinthians 2:7-9; Hebrews 10:7; Acts 9:6).

As a Child of God, your prophetic destiny is the path that the Father of all has earmarked for you or that which He has spoken or written concerning you. Some call it God's redemptive revelation, His dream, vision or purpose for your life. Furthermore, it includes your God-given abilities and place in the body of Christ.

"For I say, through the grace given unto me, to every man that is among you, not to think of himself more highly than he ought to think; but to think soberly, according as God hath dealt to every man the measure of faith. For as we have many members in one body, and all members have not the same office: So we, being many, are one body in Christ, and every one members one of another. Having then gifts differing according to the grace that is given to us, whether prophecy, let us prophesy according to the proportion of faith; Or ministry, let us wait on our ministering: or he that teacheth, on teaching; Or he that exhorteth, on exhortation: he that giveth, let him do it with simplicity; he that ruleth, with diligence; he that sheweth mercy, with cheerfulness. Let love be without dissimulation. Abhor that which is evil; cleave to that which is good."

"Wherefore he saith, when he ascended up on high, he led captivity captive, and gave gifts unto men... And he gave some, apostles; and some, prophets; and some,

evangelists; and some, pastors and teachers" (Romans 12:3-9; Ephesians 4:8, 11).

Jesus Christ's life and ministry was charted with clear direction because He found and fulfilled His prophetic destiny. In one of Christ's seven statements on the cross was, *"It is finished"* (John 19:30). In other words, I have fulfilled my prophetic destiny.

Paul's Example

This great Apostle followed the example of his Master. He was not disobedient to the heavenly vision. He was not afraid when he faced the threat of the enemies but stood his ground knowing full well that the will of God must be done even at the point of death. He remains focused and declared in 2 Timothy 4:6-8,

"For I am now ready to be offered, and the time of my departure is at hand. I have fought a good fight, I have finished my course, I have kept the faith: Henceforth there is laid up for me a crown of righteousness, which the Lord, the righteous judge, shall give me at that day: and not to me only, but unto all them also that love his appearing."

We can never know true joy until we find and fulfil our prophetic destiny. It is important to add that it is only our prophetic destiny that is worth dying for; anything that is not worth dying for is not worth living for either.

Pointers to Prophetic Destiny

"Remove not the ancient landmark, which thy fathers have set...Remove not the old landmark; and enter not into the fields of the fatherless" (Proverbs 22:28; 23:10). Pointers are like landmarks which clearly show us the field or place that God has earmarked for us. They are like road signs which direct the traveller to his destination. You can find your redemptive revelation through the following:

A. A word from the Lord - written or spoken concerning you. *"Now there were in the church that was at Antioch certain prophets and teachers; as Barnabas, and Simeon that was called Niger, and Lucius of Cyrene, and Manaen, which had been brought up with Herod the tetrarch, and Saul. As they ministered to the Lord, and fasted, the Holy Ghost said, Separate me Barnabas and Saul for the work whereunto I have called them. And when they had fasted and prayed, and laid their hands on them, they sent them away"* (Acts 13:1-3).

The Scripture is God's infallible word. Through the scripture, we can find that which has been written or spoken concerning us as believers. By His grace, we can discover some fundamental revelations about us as the children of God relating to: (i) Mission and Ministry (Matthew 28:19; Mark 16:15). (ii) Marriage (2 Corinthians 6:17-18). (iii) The Miraculous (Mark 16:17-18; John 14:12). (iv) Material blessings (Philippians 4:19; Luke 6:38; 2 Corinthians 8:9; Malachi 3:8-12). (v) The Ministry of Holy Spirit through us (Luke 24:49; Romans 8:26). These revelations are a basic rebirth of every redeemed child of God. How many of us are working in the reality of these revelations written and spoken concerning us today?

Moreover, as we bring our lives and ministries in line with the lives and ministries of Bible characters, the word can begin to give us specific pictures about our redemption revelations. Furthermore, God does speak prophetically today to show the way into our purpose in life. It is important to state that every prophetic word must conform to the Scripture. *"To the law and to the testimony: if they speak not according to this word, it is because there is no light in them"* (Isaiah 8:20).

B. Dream(s), Vision(s) and Divine Encounter. These are best illustrated through the cases of (i) Joseph (Genesis 37:51), (ii) Paul (Acts 9:3-7, 12; 16:9-10; 27:22-25), (iii) Moses (Exodus 3:1-10). On balance of the scripture, we can state that our prophetic dreams and visions are Holy Spirit-inspired and imparted (Acts 2:17; Joel

2:28).

C. The Guiding Ministry of Holy Ghost. (John 14:16-17, 26; Acts 16:6-7). One of the ministries of the Holy Ghost is divine guidance. Today's believers have not cultivated enough the discipline of listening and recognizing the voice of the Holy Spirit. This partly accounts for the lack of spiritual direction in the life many believers today. Greater maturity will come when we learn, listen to and obey the "promptings" of the Holy Spirit.

D. Prayer Matched with Divine Coincidence. Examples: Peter (Acts 10:9-20); The disciples (Acts 4:23-31); Eliezer (Genesis 24:12-21).

E. Divine Go-slow: Examples Jonah (Jonah 1:1-17; 3-4), the disciples (John 11:6, 14, 21, 37, 43-44).

F. Divine Restlessness (Jeremiah 20:9).

G. A Burning Desire or Impression (Luke 24:32).

H. Parental Influence and Covenant Heritage: Abraham (Genesis 12:1-5, 18:17-19); The Rechabites (Jeremiah 35:1-11); 2 Timothy 1:5).

I. Guidance by matured believers who themselves have clear understanding of their own redemptive revelation (1 Samuel 3:1-2; Ephesians 4:11-12).

J. Implications of our Names: Jabez (1 Chronicle 4:10);

Jesus Christ (Matthew 1:21); Abram/Abraham (Genesis 17:4-5). Believers are called Christians (Acts 11:26, 26:28; 1 Peter 4:16). Do we know the implications of that name? (Colossians 1:27; 1 John 4:4; 5:4; Revelations 1:5-6; Galatians 3:13-14, 26-29; 2 Corinthians 6:15-16, 18; 1 Corinthians 6:14-15, 19-20; John 14:12).

Promises Concerning your Prophetic Destiny

a. Isaiah 58:11, *"And the Lord shall guide thee continually ..."*

b. Isaiah 45: 2 *"I will go before thee and make the crooked place straight ..."*

c. Isaiah 45:13, *"I have raised him up in righteousness, and I will direct his ways."*

d. Isaiah 46:10, *"Declaring the end from the beginning, and from ancient times the things that are not yet done, saying, My counsel shall stand, and I will do all my pleasure."*

e. Isaiah 46:11, *"Calling a ravenous bird from the east, the man that executeth my counsel from a far country: yea, I have spoken it, I will also bring it to pass; I have purposed it, I will also do it."*

f. 2 Timothy 1:12, *"For the which cause I also suffer these things: nevertheless, I am not ashamed: for I know whom I have believed, and am persuaded that he is able to keep that which I have committed unto him against that day:*

g. 2 Corinthians 12:9, *"And he said unto me, My grace is sufficient for thee: for my strength is made perfect in weakness. Most gladly therefore will I rather glory in my infirmities, that the power of Christ may rest upon me."*

CHAPTER SIXTEEN

FULFILLING YOUR REDEMPTIVE REVELATIONS

"And say to Archippus, Take heed to the ministry which thou hast received in the Lord, that thou fulfil it... But none of these things move me, neither count I my life dear unto myself, so that I might finish my course with joy, and the ministry, which I have received of the Lord Jesus, to testify the gospel of the grace of God" (Colossians 4:17; Acts 20:24).

Apostle Paul's original signal to Archippus was very clear: *"say to Archippus, take heed to the ministry which thou hast received in the Lord, that thou fulfil it.'* This Apostolic exhortation does not imply any unfaithfulness on the part of this servant of God.

Hence, he was called a fellow soldier of Paul in Philemon 2, *"And to our beloved Apphia, and Archippus our fellowsoldier, and to the church in thy house."* Here, Paul reminds him to see, as it were, his ministry in the Colossian Church as coming from God and to ensure that this redemptive revelation was fulfilled. This means it was possible for Archippus not to fulfil his God-given dreams and ministry.

It is very significant that Paul singles him out for this powerful exhortation. Why? You may ask. It was because this ministry was God's unique calling on Archippus which no one else can fulfil but himself in the whole economy of God. Despite bonds and afflictions, Paul affirmed his commitment to the fulfilment of God's calling in Acts 20:24. It is, therefore, one thing to know that our God-given visions, dreams and redemptive revelations are entirely crucial things which require us paying the price to fulfil our divine destiny.

Why You Must Fulfil Your Divine Destiny?

"After a long time the lord of those servants cometh, and reckoneth with them. And so he that had received five talents came and brought other five talents, saying, Lord, thou deliveredst unto me five talents: behold, I have gained beside them five talents more. His lord said unto him, Well done, thou good and faithful servant: thou hast

been faithful over a few things, I will make thee ruler over many things: enter thou into the joy of thy lord. He also that had received two talents came and said, Lord, thou deliveredst unto me two talents: behold, I have gained two other talents beside them. His lord said unto him, Well done, good and faithful servant; thou hast been faithful over a few things, I will make thee ruler over many things: enter thou into the joy of thy lord...Wherefore we labour, that, whether present or absent, we may be accepted of him. For we must all appear before the judgment seat of Christ; that every one may receive the things done in his body, according to that he hath done, whether it be good or bad."* (Matthew 25:19-23)

The purpose of our existence is our divine destiny which is primarily to glorify God. This begins with reconciling with Him personally by salvation through Jesus Christ and living for Him at all times. Secondarily, after salvation, we are supposed to go to Heaven immediately but God decided to preserve us alive on earth to lead others to Christ by means of the gospel of truth with everything we have our time, talents and the Holy Ghost, whatever our calling.

Once this is done, we would have fulfilled our ministry and there would be no need to overstay our sojourn in the world. So, God will take us home into eternity either by death or the rapture to receive the rewards of our assignment whatever our age. Listen to Apostle Paul, a man of like passion as we are, who completed his mission on earth and knew it:

"But watch thou in all things, endure afflictions, do the work of an evangelist, make full proof of thy ministry. For I am now ready to be offered, and the time of my departure is at hand. I have fought a good fight, I have finished my course, I have kept the faith: Henceforth there is laid up for me a crown of righteousness, which the Lord, the righteous judge, shall give me at that day: and not to me only, but unto all them also that love his appearing." (2 Timothy 4:5-8)

"We then, as workers together with him, beseech you also that ye receive not the grace of God in vain" (2 Corinthians 6:1). God predestined us to adoption as sons/daughters by Jesus Christ; therefore, we must allow Him and cooperate with Him to guide us through the process of bringing to birth His perfect will for our lives.

How Do We Fulfil God's Purpose for Our Lives?

"Before I formed thee in the belly I knew thee; and before thou camest forth out of the womb I sanctified thee, and I ordained thee a prophet unto the nations...Thine eyes did see my substance, yet being unperfect; and in thy book all my members were written, which in continuance were fashioned, when as yet there was none of them...For we are his workmanship, created in Christ Jesus unto good works, which God hath before ordained that we should

walk in them." (Jeremiah 1:5; Psalm 139:16; Ephesians 2:10)

The following are practical steps to take in fulfilling the purpose of God for our lives Perceive, Believe, Conceive, Achieve and Receive.

Perceive

"And he brought him forth abroad, and said, Look now toward heaven, and tell the stars, if thou be able to number them: and he said unto him, So shall thy seed be. And he believed in the Lord; and he counted it to him for righteousness… And in them is fulfilled the prophecy of Esaias, which saith, By hearing ye shall hear, and shall not understand; and seeing ye shall see, and shall not perceive" (Genesis 15:5-6; Matthew 13:14). To perceive is to know properly, to ascertain, to discover and be made to know. This implies understanding beyond the surface of a thing. What do you see of yourself as a believer? You will be what you perceive. As David, you have to perceive yourself as a giant-killer and your Goliath will fall. Perceive yourself as more than a conqueror and like Paul, you will fight a good fight of faith and prevail ultimately.

Believe

"And he believed in the Lord; and he counted it to him for righteousness…But without faith it is impossible to please him: for he that cometh to God must believe that he is, and that he is a rewarder of them that diligently seek him" (Genesis 15:6;

Hebrews 11:6). Faith in God is the activator of your God-given dream. Consider Joseph and his brothers. They did not believe his dreams because they were envious and plotted to kill him. But Joseph believed what God has revealed unto him and realized it contained a great eternal purpose, divine destiny and an original intention God has to salvage the whole nation in the future. Joseph refused to cast away his confidence which hath great recompense of reward (Hebrews 10:35). The fact that Joseph stood for something, he refused to fall for anything, not even the free offer of Potiphar's wife. You must believe in your God-given revelations, otherwise, you will fall for anything that comes across your way.

Conceive

"Therefore I say unto you, What things soever ye desire, when ye pray, believe that ye receive them, and ye shall have them… I can do all things through Christ which strengtheneth me" (Mark 11:24; Philippians 4:13). If you perceived what you know God wants you to be and have believed it, it is important that you carry it as a divine pregnancy and guide it so that it doesn't get aborted. Conception is the proper articulation of our dream in such a way that a clear picture of it could be imagined. Think about an elegant high rise building? It was conceived by an architect. With the help of an engineer, everything was documented and became a masterpiece. Likewise, with God on your side, everything is possible. The Holy Spirit will convey to

your heart God's blueprint and guide you through to the point of actualization.

Achieve

"Seest thou a man diligent in his business? he shall stand before kings; he shall not stand before mean men...The hand of the diligent shall bear rule: but the slothful shall be under tribute...For we hear that there are some which walk among you disorderly, working not at all, but are busybodies. Now them that are such we command and exhort by our Lord Jesus Christ, that with quietness they work, and eat their own bread" (Proverbs 22:29; 12:24; 2 Thessalonians 3:11-12).

Many dreams are never born because their dreamers do nothing about them. One universal truth is this: dreams without achievement make you a day-dreamer. Do you have a dream to be an intercessor? Then, set time to pray. If your dream is being an evangelist, please, go out for personal evangelism. While Joseph served diligently under his father's house, in Potiphar's house and in the prison, his gift made room for him; though a stranger, he was moved from prison to the palace in Egypt to become prime minister. If you want to achieve your redemptive revelations and realize your dreams and visions in life, you must be ready to pay the price. The price you need to pay is hard work. This will entail decision, denial, determination, dedication, development, discipline and directed prayers unto God.

Decision *"And Jabez was more honourable than his brethren: and his mother called his name Jabez, saying, Because I bare him with sorrow. And Jabez called on the God of Israel, saying, Oh that thou wouldest bless me indeed, and enlarge my coast, and that thine hand might be with me, and that thou wouldest keep me from evil, that it may not grieve me! And God granted him that which he requested"* (1 Chronicles 4:9-10). Grace to take firm a decision that is in harmony with our God-given dream and vision is what we need to pray for.

Denial *"Lest there be any fornicator, or profane person, as Esau, who for one morsel of meat sold his birthright. For ye know how that afterward, when he would have inherited the blessing, he was rejected: for he found no place of repentance, though he sought it carefully with tears…But what things were gain to me, those I counted loss for Christ. Yea doubtless, and I count all things but loss for the excellency of the knowledge of Christ Jesus my Lord: for whom I have suffered the loss of all things, and do count them but dung, that I may win Christ"* (Hebrews 12:16-17; Philippians 3:7-8). We must deny ourselves of temporary pleasures even if they are legitimate in order to realize our birthright.

Dedication *"Whatsoever thy hand findeth to do, do it with thy might; for there is no work, nor device, nor knowledge, nor wisdom, in the grave, whither thou goest…And I will very gladly spend and be spent for you; though the more abundantly*

Fulfilling Your Redemptive Revelations

I love you, the less I be loved" (Ecclesiastes 9:10; 2 Corinthians 12:15). Dedicate your energy, exploit your talents and deploy your skills with all your ability towards actualizing your divinely-guided goals to achieve your dream.

Determination - Determination is one quality that will keep you going should the going get tough. It is a rare attribute used only once in the entire scripture. *"Therefore wait ye upon me, saith the Lord, until the day that I rise up to the prey: for my determination is to gather the nations, that I may assemble the kingdoms, to pour upon them mine indignation, even all my fierce anger: for all the earth shall be devoured with the fire of my jealousy"* (Zephaniah 3:8).

Development - *"Study to shew thyself approved unto God, a workman that needeth not to be ashamed, rightly dividing the word of truth"* (2 Timothy 2:15). You must study, research and read wide so as to garner relevant information that must be applied wisely to develop yourselves in order to realize your life dreams. *"Till I come, give attendance to reading, to exhortation, to doctrine."* (1 Timothy 4:13)

Discipline - *"I therefore so run, not as uncertainly; so fight I, not as one that beateth the air: But I keep under my body, and bring it into subjection: lest that by any means, when I have preached to others, I myself should be a castaway...He openeth* *also their ear to discipline, and commandeth that they return from iniquity"* (1Corinthians 9:26-27; Job 36:10). Discipline involves controlled use of our time and talents to produce moral or mental improvement. You may only consolidate your survival and sustenance of your dreams by discipline which involves cutting down your excesses in spending, sleep, consumption, luxury and other legitimacies

Directed Prayers - *"Then answered I them, and said unto them, The God of heaven, he will prosper us; therefore we his servants will arise and build: but ye have no portion, nor right, nor memorial, in Jerusalem"* (Nehemiah 2:20). Through Spirit-directed prayers, we receive grace, strength and power to pursue our redemptive revelations and fulfil them.

Receive

"Cast not away therefore your confidence, which hath great recompence of reward.[6] For ye have need of patience, that, after ye have done the will of God, ye might receive the promise. For yet a little while, and he that shall come will come, and will not tarry. And Pharaoh said unto his servants, Can we find such a one as this is, a man in whom the Spirit of God is?" (Hebrews 10:35-37; Genesis 41:38). Look at the day Joseph's life was turned around; he crossed from prison to the palace, from a servant to being served. The powerless became a power broker. Surely, that which we perceive and believe, which

we conceive and seek to achieve, we shall receive through obedience to His word of vision.

Destroying the Stronghold of 'No' in Destiny

"And I will make Pathros desolate, and will set fire in Zoan, and will execute judgments in No. And I will pour my fury upon Sin, the strength of Egypt; and I will cut off the multitude of No. And I will set fire in Egypt: Sin shall have great pain, and No shall be rent asunder, and Noph shall have distresses daily ... The Lord of hosts, the God of Israel, saith; Behold, I will punish the multitude of No, and Pharaoh, and Egypt, with their gods, and their kings; even Pharaoh, and all them that trust in him ... Art thou better than populous No, that was situate among the rivers, that had the waters round about it, whose rampart was the sea, and her wall was from the sea Ethiopia and Egypt were her strength, and it was infinite; Put and Lubim were thy helpers" (Ezekiel 30:14-16; Jeremiah 46:25; Nahum 3:8-9).

No was a city in Egypt that was well-fortified and popular. It was an infinite city with a negative attitude to God's righteousness, therefore, God pronounced judgment on her. Symbolically, No is negative, never, not now, impossibility and unlimited suffering which are roadblocks to human progress and success. There are many 'NOES' in many lives today - poverty, hard luck, failure, sicknesses, separation, divorce, defeat, deaths, curses, hindrances, blockages, destiny destroyers, demonic attacks among others. They are destiny destroyers that try to hinder us from fulfilling our prophetic destiny as they remain mountains and appear unmovable. But God says, He will cut off the multitude of No and No shall be rent asunder.

"For the weapons of our warfare are not carnal, but mighty through God to the pulling down of strong holds;) Casting down imaginations, and every high thing that exalteth itself against the knowledge of God, and bringing into captivity every thought to the obedience of Christ; And having in a readiness to revenge all disobedience, when your obedience is fulfilled" (2 Corinthians 10:4-6).

A stronghold is any fortified place that satan builds to exalt himself against the knowledge and plans of God for our destiny. Thank God for His manifold promises that are yea and amen and full of hope! All the negatives, never and not now, can be settled with God in prayers.

"And it shall come to pass in that day, that his burden shall be taken away from off thy shoulder, and his yoke from off thy neck, and the yoke shall be destroyed because of the anointing…Awake, awake; put on thy strength, O Zion; put on thy beautiful garments, O Jerusalem, the holy city: for henceforth there shall no more come into thee the uncircumcised

and the unclean. Shake thyself from the dust; arise, and sit down, O Jerusalem: loose thyself from the bands of thy neck, O captive daughter of Zion" (Isaiah 10:27; 52:1-2).

No are destiny breakers and they are identifiable. Some are self-induced; others are people-imparted, while more are enemy-inspired.

Discerning Personal Strongholds

Personal strongholds can be identified by:

a. "Knowing thyself": This is the wise counsel of an ancient philosopher of the eighth century bc called Socrates who said, "To know thyself is the beginning of wisdom." He summarily opined that knowing oneself requires self-examination, but not in a sense that would come most naturally to contemporary readers. Instead, self-examination as understood by Socrates requires investigating, through debate and dialogue, the contours of concepts that seem necessary for living a good life: knowledge, justice, virtue, piety, and the like.

This is much in tandem with the biblical submission that *"The fear of the LORD is the beginning of wisdom:… and the knowledge of the holy is understanding."* (Psalm 111:10; Proverbs 9:10). So, to know yourself or appreciate your personal identity, you must understand what personal strongholds are and overcome them. Personal strongholds are those things which Satan inspires to influence one's personal life negatively. These include personal sins, thoughts or worldview, feelings, attitudes and behavioural patterns. Thus knowing yourself is knowing and appraising your depravity as a sinner and accepting the appeal of the propitiation of Christ's sacrifice for human redemption so as not to get lost in some needless, foolhardy, atheistic or religious arrogance and perdition ultimately.

b. Personal sin: *"But the fearful, and unbelieving, and the abominable, and murderers, and whoremongers, and sorcerers, and idolaters, and all liars, shall have their part in the lake which burneth with fire and brimstone: which is the second death"* (Revelation 21:8; Also, read Romans 1:29-32 and Galatians 5:19-21).

c. Wrong thought pattern or worldview: *"For as he thinketh in his heart, so is he: Eat and drink, saith he to thee; but his heart is not with thee…And be not conformed to this world: but be ye transformed by the renewing of your mind, that ye may prove what is that good, and acceptable, and perfect, will of God"* (Proverbs 23:7; Romans 12:2).

d. Feelings of dependency, despair, inability and complexes: *"But the men that went up with him said, We be not able to go up against the people; for they are stronger than we…And there we saw the giants, the sons of Anak, which come of the giants: and we were in our own sight as grasshoppers, and so we were in their sight"* (Numbers 13:31, 33).

e. Negative attitudes and behavioural patterns: "*Go to the ant, thou sluggard; consider her ways, and be wise: Which having no guide, overseer, or ruler, Provideth her meat in the summer, and gathereth her food in the harvest. How long wilt thou sleep, O sluggard? when wilt thou arise out of thy sleep? Yet a little sleep, a little slumber, a little folding of the hands to sleep: So shall thy poverty come as one that travelleth, and thy want as an armed man…Not slothful in business; fervent in spirit; serving the Lord*" (Proverbs 6:6-11; Romans 12:11). Lack of focus.

Demolishing Personal Strongholds

Once identified, personal strongholds can be destroyed when you:

a. Confront yourself with the reality and consequences of your personal sin. "*He that covereth his sins shall not prosper: but whoso confesseth and forsaketh them shall have mercy… For the wages of sin is death; but the gift of God is eternal life through Jesus Christ our Lord*" (Proverbs 28:13; Romans 6:23).

b. Confess all known sins repentantly. "*If we confess our sins, he is faithful and just to forgive us our sins, and to cleanse us from all unrighteousness*" (1 John 1:9).

c. Close all doorways that give the enemy access to building strongholds in your life. "*He that diggeth a pit shall fall into it; and whoso breaketh an hedge, a serpent shall bite him"* (Ecclesiastes 10:8).

d. Come violently against any identified stronghold and strongman. *"And from the days of John the Baptist until now the kingdom of heaven suffereth violence, and the violent take it by force....See, I have this day set thee over the nations and over the kingdoms, to root out, and to pull down, and to destroy, and to throw down, to build, and to plant"* (Matthew 11:12; Jeremiah 1:10).

e. Conquer destiny-destroying feelings, attitudes and behaviours with destiny-developing ones such as replacing laziness with hard work and slothfulness with assiduity. *"Seest thou a man diligent in his business? he shall stand before kings; he shall not stand before mean men"* (Proverbs 22:29).

f. Cast away the garment of unbelief, fear and negative confession. *"Say unto them, As truly as I live, saith the LORD, as ye have spoken in mine ears, so will I do to you:"* (Numbers 14:28).

g. Consider the wonders of your God and give Him praise, worship and adoration. *"The stone which the builders refused is become the head stone of the corner. This is the Lord's doing; it is marvellous in our eyes. This is the day which the Lord hath made; we will rejoice and be glad in it...I will praise thee; for I am fearfully and wonderfully made: marvellous are thy works; and that my soul knoweth right well"* (Psalms 118:22-24; 139:14).

Fulfilling Your Redemptive Revelations

Developing a Destiny-Fulfilling Disposition

a. Say to yourself, "*I can do all things through Christ which strengtheneth me*" (Philippians 4:13). It is not humility to say you cannot when the word says you can.

b. Tell yourself, "it is possible." "*Jesus said unto him, If thou canst believe, all things are possible to him that believeth*" (Mark 9:23).

c. Have a mountain-desire. "*Now therefore give me this mountain, whereof the Lord spake in that day; for thou heardest in that day how the Anakims were there, and that the cities were great and fenced: if so be the Lord will be with me, then I shall be able to drive them out, as the Lord said*" (Joshua 14:12). Why settle in the valley of defeat and mediocrity when you can ask God for your own mountain as Caleb did?

d. Take a decisive action. "*And Caleb drove thence the three sons of Anak, Sheshai, and Ahiman, and Talmai, the children of Anak*" (Joshua 15:14). If your mountain does not come to you, go for your mountain. A journey of 1,000 kilometers begins with a single step taken in a day! "*Now is the acceptable time … now is the day of salvation*" (2 Corinthians 6:2).

e. Develop a deep consciousness of the bigness of our God. God is a big God. The difference between David and Saul was that while Saul saw the mightiness of Goliath, David beheld the Almightiness of the God of

Israel. *"And Saul said to David, Thou art not able to go against this Philistine to fight with him: for thou art but a youth, and he a man of war from his youth…Then said David to the Philistine, Thou comest to me with a sword, and with a spear, and with a shield: but I come to thee in the name of the Lord of hosts, the God of the armies of Israel, whom thou hast defied. This day will the Lord deliver thee into mine hand; and I will smite thee, and take thine head from thee; and I will give the carcases of the host of the Philistines this day unto the fowls of the air, and to the wild beasts of the earth; that all the earth may know that there is a God in Israel. And all this assembly shall know that the Lord saveth not with sword and spear: for the battle is the Lord's, and he will give you into our hand"* (1 Samuel 17:33, 45-47).

f. Always remember that God can do it again. *"And David said unto Saul, Thy servant kept his father's sheep, and there came a lion, and a bear, and took a lamb out of the flock: And I went out after him, and smote him, and delivered it out of his mouth: and when he arose against me, I caught him by his beard, and smote him, and slew him. Thy servant slew both the lion and the bear: and this uncircumcised Philistine shall be as one of them, seeing he hath defied the armies of the living God. David said moreover, The Lord that delivered me out of the paw of the lion, and out of the paw of the bear, he will deliver me out of the hand of this Philistine. And Saul said unto David, Go, and the Lord be with thee"* (1 Samuel 17: 34-37).

Fulfilling Your Redemptive Revelations

When the foregoing are put in place, it becomes easy to fulfil the purpose of our creation or the essence of our existence which answers perhaps life's toughest question, Why am I here?

Email prayer requests and praise reports to: akindewum@gmail.com

PRECEPTS FOR ALL

- Teaching them to observe all things whatsoever I have commanded you: and, lo, I am with you always, even unto the end of the world. Amen Matthew 28:20
- And he said unto them, Go ye into all the world, and preach the gospel to every creature. -Mark 16:15
- Judge not, and ye shall not be judged: condemn not, and ye shall not be condemned: forgive, and ye shall be forgiven: But I have prayed for thee, that thy faith fail not: and when thou art converted, strengthen thy brethren. -Luke 6:37; 22:32
- This is my commandment, That ye love one another, as I have loved you. - John 15:12
- Take heed therefore unto yourselves, and to all the flock, over the which the Holy Ghost hath made you overseers, to feed the church of God, which he hath purchased with his own blood. - Acts 20:28
- Let love be without dissimulation. Abhor that which is evil; cleave to that which is good. Be kindly affectioned one to another with brotherly love; in honour preferring one another; Not

slothful in business; fervent in spirit; serving the Lord; Rejoicing in hope; patient in tribulation; continuing instant in prayer. Romans 12:9-12
- Give none offence, neither to the Jews, nor to the Gentiles, nor to the church of God. - 1 Corinthians 10:32
- But he that glorieth, let him glory in the Lord. For not he that commendeth himself is approved, but whom the Lord commendeth. - 2 Corinthians 10:17-18
- Bear ye one another's burdens, and so fulfil the law of Christ. Galatians 6:2
- Let nothing be done through strife or vainglory; but in lowliness of mind let each esteem other better than themselves. Philippians 2:3
- Let the word of Christ dwell in you richly in all wisdom; teaching and admonishing one another in psalms and hymns and spiritual songs, singing with grace in your hearts to the Lord. Colossians 3:16
- Prove all things; hold fast that which is good. Abstain from all appearance of evil. And the very God of peace sanctify you wholly; and I pray God your whole spirit and soul and body be preserved blameless unto the coming of our Lord Jesus Christ. 1 Thessalonians 5:21-23
- But ye, brethren, be not weary in well doing. 2

Thessalonians 3:13
- Let no man despise thy youth; but be thou an example of the believers, in word, in conversation, in charity, in spirit, in faith, in purity. 1 Timothy 4:12
- Study to shew thyself approved unto God, a workman that needeth not to be ashamed, rightly dividing the word of truth. 2 Timothy 2:15
- That the communication of thy faith may become effectual by the acknowledging of every good thing which is in you in Christ Jesus. Philemon 6
- Follow peace with all men, and holiness, without which no man shall see the Lord. - Hebrews 12:14
- Casting all your care upon him; for he careth for you. 1 Peter 5:7
- But grow in grace, and in the knowledge of our Lord and Saviour Jesus Christ. To him be glory both now and for ever. Amen. 2 Peter 3:18
- Love not the world, neither the things that are in the world. If any man love the world, the love of the Father is not in him. - 1 John 2:15
- We therefore ought to receive such, that we might be fellowhelpers to the truth. - 3 John 8
- Behold, I come quickly: hold that fast which thou hast, that no man take thy crown. - Revelation 3:11
- Let integrity and uprightness preserve me; for I wait on thee. - Psalms 25:21

- "Humility and patience are the surest proofs of the increase of love." - **John Wesley**
- "Christians can never sin cheaply; they pay a heavy price for iniquity. Transgression destroys peace of mind, obscures fellowship with Jesus, hinders prayer, brings darkness over the soul; therefore be not the serf and bondman of sin." **C. H. Spurgeon**
- "Nobody ever outgrows Scripture; the book widens and deepens with our years." **C. H. Spurgeon**.
- "We are the Bibles the world is reading; we are the creeds the world is needing; we are the sermons the world is heeding." - **Billy Graham**
- "How can you expect to dwell with God forever, if you so neglect and forsake him here?" — **Jonathan Edward**

EPILOGUE

The Book, "VICTORIOUS CHRISTIAN LIVING ESSENTIALS," exposes you to the way of salvation and holiness, godliness, righteous living and victory over temptation and persecution. We are saved to serve God in His Kingdom on earth until Christ comes. There are many things you will learn in this book that directs and guides you with Bible principles and references needed to overcome. Everything needed for our victory are links to the unfailing word of God. There are provisions for our victory over sins, self, world, enemies and satan. It is possible for us to fulfil our prophetic destiny through obedience and leading of the Holy Spirit. It is expected of us to be victorious in our Christian journey with fruits in the face of the challenges of life that we face daily in peril, tribulation, sicknesses, destitution, lack or poverty. Entrance into God's presence with absolute trust and obedience to His word makes difference and paves way for our victory. Our Christian life is birthed by prayers and all that pertain to godliness. Also, we overcome the devil daily by God's word and prayers. Jesus is coming very soon and we need to prepare for His second coming for the prepared Saints; hence, we must continue to the very end and fight a good fight of faith to keep our victories.

BIBLIOGRAPHY

Hitchcock, Roswell D. (1871) *Hitchcock's New and Complete Analysis of the Holy Bible.* (New York: A.J. Johnson).

Mitchell S. Green (2018) *Know Thyself: The Value and Limits of Self-Knowledge.* (New York and London: Routledge, Taylor and Francis Group), pp. 11 & 25.

Napoleon Hill (1937) *Think and Grow Rich: A Black Choice.* (Unite States of America: The Ralston Society)

Stephen Smith (2019) *A Deeper Look at What the Bible Says about Spiritual Growth.* Openbible.info

The Gutenberg Bible (1455) *A Latin Language Bible* (Mainz, Germany).

The Holy Bible (1611) *King James Version.* Trinitarian Bible Society, England (1991). (Cambridge University Press: Cambridge).

Further Reading

Johnson, P. (2011) *Socrates: A Man for Our Times* (London: Viking). Accessible and well-written biography of Socrates.

Kraut, R. (2009) 'The Examined Life,' in S. Ahbel-Rapp and R. Kamtakar (eds.) *A Companion to Socrates* (Hoboken, NJ: Wiley-Blackwell), pp. 22842. Argues for a more modest reading of the Socratic Dictum than is normally invoked.

Internet Resources

Green, 'The Examined Life,' in Wi-Phi (http://wi-phi.org). A brief animated video briefly setting forth the core ideas of this chapter.

https://archive.org/details/hitchcocksnewco00hitc

https://books.google.com.ng/books?id=AdxdDwAAQBAJ&dq=Thomas+Buxton:+You+know+the+value+of+prayer%3B+its+precious+beyond+all+price.+Never,+never+neglect+it.&source=gbs_navlinks_s

https://en.wikipedia.org/wiki/Know_thyself. Socrates ("Know thyself", quoting Pythia, the Oracle of Delphi).

Https://hisdeeplove.wordpress.com

Nails, D. 'Socrates,' in *The Stanford Encyclopedia of Philosophy* (http://plato.stanford.edu/entries/socrates/). Accessible and informative overview of Socrates' life and thought.

Power BibleCD program © 2000 Phil Lindner, Online Publishing Inc., Michigan. (Version 2.5 KJV). bible@mail.com

www.brainyquote.com/quote/denis_waitley_130424

www.gutenberg-bible.com

www.ingramcontent.com/pod-product-compliance
Lightning Source LLC
Chambersburg PA
CBHW071457040426
42444CB00008B/1387